MW00891616

MacBook Air
Guide

The Ultimate Guide for
MacBook Air & macOS

Welcome

The MacBook Air is a beautiful computer, with the thinnest design in Apple's lineup of notebooks. Its iconic wedge is created from 100 percent recycled aluminum, and it comes in three attractive colors: Silver, Space Grey, and Gold. These are just a few of the reasons why you'll see so many MacBook Air's in coffee shops, airports and lecture halls. They also explain why the MacBook Air is Apple's most loved Mac.

Anyone who has used a Mac before will feel at home on the MacBook Air, but for those who grew up with touch devices like the iPhone, or those who have always used Windows-based PCs, the MacBook Air can be intimidating to learn and understand. This book is here to help you understand the MacBook Air, from its very basics — such as setting up Wi-Fi — to it's most advanced features, like recovering deleted files or creating drive partitions. You'll also learn about the macOS operating system, what to do if you have a hardware problem, plus much more.

Turn over the page and you'll find the book contents, which provides a brief glance at what you can expect to find in each chapter. Alternatively, jump to the back of the book to see a more detailed index.

Just before I go, if there's anything you would like to know that isn't covered in this book, send me an email at tom@leafpublishing.co.uk, and I'll be more than happy to help.

Tom Rudderham
Author
tom@leafpublishing.co.uk

Credits:

Author: Tom Rudderham
Editor: Zeljko Jurancevic
Copy Editor: Kaye Inglis

Published by:
Leaf Publishing LTD
www.leafpublishing.co.uk

ISBN:
9781791974527

Contents

Welcome

The Basics

36
Talk to Siri

Mouse, Trackpad, & Keyboard

61
Discover emojis
and accents

Customise Your MacBook

62
Choose a new
wallpaper

99
Learn how to edit your photos

111
Explore the world in 3D

Terminology

Wondering what all those words and phrases mean?

The MacBook Air is a state of the art piece of equipment, so perhaps it's inevitable that talking about it involves using a wide-ranging assortment of words, phrases, and terminology. In this book, you're going to hear a lot about the MacBook hardware, software, and features. Don't worry, each one of them will be explained as we go, so you'll never feel confused or get lost halfway through a paragraph. To get you started, here are a few of the words we will be using constantly throughout this book...

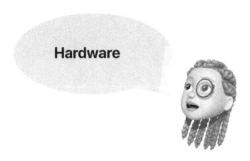

Hardware

Whenever the word hardware is used, we're basically talking about the MacBook in its physical form. The thing which sits on your lap.

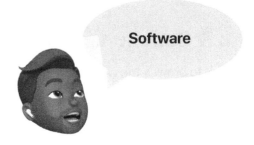

Software

Think of software as a set of instructions for doing something on your MacBook Air. These instructions might be millions of words long, and they were probably written by a large team of people. To most humans, it's utter gibberish. It looks something like this:

```
int main(int argc, char * argv[]) {
    @autoreleasepool {
        return UIApplicationMain( argc, argv, nil,
NSStringFromClass( [AVCamAppDelegate
class] ) );
    }
```

To a programmer who writes in Swift (Apple's programming language), this makes perfect sense. It's just a fraction of the code required to tell your MacBook how to capture an image using its camera. The full piece of code is tens of thousands of lines long.

App

The word app is short for application. An application is a piece of software, separate from macOS, which lets you do something. There's an app on your MacBook for browsing the web. There's an app for sending messages. There's an app for looking at your photos. I'm sure you get the idea.

macOS

This is the name of the software which powers your MacBook Air. It's one of the most complicated pieces of software ever created by man. It tells your Mac how to turn on, how to take a photo, how to browse the internet, how to scan your fingerprint when you want to unlock your Mac plus so much more. It can also learn over time. macOS will learn about your habits, how you type to individual people, where you travel, and what you sound like. It uses all of this learning to help you type quicker, find photos quicker, and basically use your Mac in a more efficient manner.

You don't have to worry about security either, because all of this personal information is fully encrypted, and the really important stuff, like your fingerprint, never leaves your Mac.

When most people think of the word macOS, they imagine the desktop on their Mac. You can think of it like that too, but really it's so much more.

Third-party apps

These are apps created by companies other than Apple. There are tens of thousands of them, and each app serves its own purpose. For example, using Photoshop you can edit photos professionally, while an app like Sketch enables you to design mobile apps. You'll find all of these apps in the...

App Store

Think of the App Store as a market for apps. Some apps are free, others cost a few dollars/pounds/euros. Some apps look like they are free, but ask for a payment to do something (this is called an "In-App Purchase"). You can find the App Store on your MacBook. It has a bright blue icon with an abstract "A" in the middle.

Encryption

Think of encryption as a padlock for words, but instead of 0-9 on the padlock, it's A-Z, plus 0-9. The software on your Mac uses encryption all the time. Whenever you send a message to a friend, all the letters you type are scrambled up, sent to the other person, then de-scrambled on their device. The same goes for video calls you make using FaceTime, your credit card's details when you check out on the internet, and much more. Nearly everything you do on your Mac is encrypted.

iCloud

Think of iCloud as a computer somewhere in the world where your photos, messages, apps, and settings are stored. Your Mac talks to this computer over the internet every day to backup new photos, send new messages, and check for updates.

Terminology continued

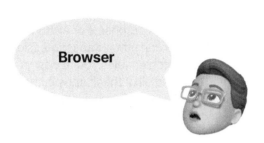

Browser

This is the term used to describe an app for navigating the internet. On the Mac, the "browser "is called Safari, but there are other browsers available to install from the App Store, such as Chrome, Firefox, and Microsoft Edge.

Restart

The word "restart" is used when something needs to be turned off, then back on again. Maybe your Mac needs to be restarted because it has stopped working, or similarly an app might need to be restarted.

Siri

Think of Siri as a virtual assistant that you can talk too. You can ask Siri what the weather is like, directions to somewhere, basic math questions, or even the answers to trivia.

Storage

Your Mac comes with a limited amount of space for storing photos, videos, apps, and other content. When you bought your Mac, you needed to choose how much storage it had available, and the more storage space you chose, the more expensive it was to buy.

Sleep

You can put your MacBook to sleep by closing the lid. When it's asleep, it will still check for new messages, emails, and notifications, but it won't use much power. In sleep mode, your Mac can last for nearly a week on a full battery charge, while in normal use (when the screen is on), it's somewhere inbetween 10 and 20 hours.

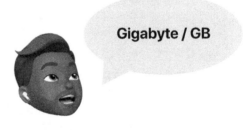

Gigabyte / GB

This storage comes in gigabytes (AKA GB), with the base MacBook Air coming with 256GB of storage.

To put that into context, you can typically save around 250 photos per gigabyte, or approximately 10 minutes of video.

Settings

You can heavily configure how your MacBook notifies you of new messages, how bright the screen is, how loud the speakers are, and even how apps track your location. These configurations are called "settings', and to make any of these changes (plus much more), then you need to open the System Preferences app.

Gestures

When we talk about gestures on the MacBook, we're referring to the use of your fingers to initiate an action on the trackpad below the keyboard. Let's say you want to zoom into a photo. The gesture to do this would be to place two fingers on the trackpad then move them apart.

Desktop

The Desktop is the first place you see after unlocking your Mac. Most of the time it's just a wallpaper image, with the Dock at the bottom of the screen, and the Apple Menu at the top, but you can add folders and files on the Desktop and then use it as a place to store things for quick access.

Attachments

If you receive an email that includes a photo, video, or document, then it is usually referred too as an attachment.

Icon

Don't understand another term?

Feel free to email Tom, the author of this book at tom@leafpublishing.co.uk, and he'll be happy to explain any further terms or phrases that you're unsure about.

The small image that represents an app is usually referred too as an "icon". It's basically a small image that when clicked on, let's you open an app, or initiate an action.

MacBook Air: hardware overview

A brief look at the MacBook Air's main features...

1 Camera
Using this camera, you can make video calls or take a photo of yourself.

2 Display
The MacBook Air's pin-sharp display shows text and videos with vivid clarity.

3 Keyboard
The keyboard is fully backlit, ensuring you can continue to type in low-light or the dark. In the top-right corner is the Touch ID button, which enables you to use your fingerprint to confirm your identity or make purchases.

4 Microphone
Tucked away in the top-corner of the keyboard is a small microphone.

5 USB-C ports
Using these two ports, you can plug other devices into the MacBook Air, such as memory cards, iPhones, or even an external monitor. This is also where you insert the power cable.

6 Trackpad
Use this trackpad to move the cursor around the screen. You can also perform Multi-Touch gestures with your fingers.

MacBook Air: keyboard overview

A quick overview of the keyboard rows and shortcuts...

Brightness
Press F1 to increase the brightness of the display, or F2 to reduce it.

Mission Control
Press F3 to open Mission Control, which enables you to quickly move between working spaces.

Launchpad
Press F4 to quickly access all of the apps installed on your Mac.

Keyboard Brightness
Adjust the brightness of the keyboard backlight with F5 and F6.

Audio playback
Press F7 to rewind or jump to the previous item. Press F8 to play and pause music. Press F9 to fast-forward through audio or skip to the next item.

Volume Controls
Press F10 to decrease the volume level, F11 to increase it, and F12 to mute the audio.

Power and Touch ID button
Press and hold this button to turn on your Mac. This button also acts as a fingerprint sensor, enabling you to confirm your identity and pay for items using Apple Pay.

Function Key
Some apps still support traditional function keys (F1 - F12). Hold down this button then press a function key, and it will work like a standard function key, rather than a shortcut.

Modifier Keys
Press Shift to type capital letters or symbols. Press Option or Command to perform keyboard shortcuts.

11

MacBook Air: in detail

When Steve Jobs took to the stage on January 15th, 2008, to announce the original MacBook Air, there were literal gasps of shock from the attending members of press.

Not because it was the thinnest laptop ever announced — although that certainly contributed to the reaction — but because of the way it was announced. Steve had an uncanny way of unveiling products. Sometimes a new Mac would rise from a plinth, other times it would be hidden under a silk cloth. For the MacBook Air, Steve had hidden it inside a standard manila envelope. The kind you see in every office across the U.K. By sliding it out of a piece of office stationary that usually holds a few sheets of paper, Steve had instantly demonstrated just how thin the MacBook Air was. It was one of his best showman moments. One that journalists still remember to this day.

The MacBook Air went on to redefine the laptop industry in a number of ways. It introduced the term "ultrabook", which was used to describe an incredibly thin, wedge-shaped laptop. It proved that powerful laptops didn't need to be bulky and heavy, and it brought all-day battery life to laptops. The Air truly embraced the notion that less can often be more.

Ten years later, the MacBook Air has been completely redesigned. It's still Apple's thinnest laptop (although not the lightest), and it will still fit inside a manila envelope, but it introduces a stunning Retina display, Touch ID, faster components, and a more modern design language.

Every part of the Air has been redesigned and re-engineered. Every detail has a remarkable fit and finish, and it's beautiful to behold.

Display

For years, the number one request from customers had been a Retina display. It was easy to understand why. The MacBook Air had been stuck with the same low-resolution screen for a decade. One that displayed jagged text, and where individual pixels could be seen by the eye.

In 2019, Apple finally brought a sharper "Retina" display to the MacBook Air. It's still 13.3-inches in diametre, but the pixel count has now been increased from 1440x900 to 2560x1600. That's four times the resolution, making everything on-screen look sharper and more beautiful. It's not just resolution that has been improved, because the MacBook Air also displays 48% more colour range than before, so images are more lifelike than ever before.

13.3"
high-resolution Retina display

True Tone technology

Razor-sharp text clarity

48%
more colours than the non-Retina model

13

Apple M1 Chip

The MacBook Air might appear to be a thin and light notebook, but inside its aluminium frame is one of the most remarkable, and powerful processors available. Called the Apple M1 chip, it's packed with an astonishing 16 billion transistors, and integrates the CPU, GPU, Neural Engine, I/O and much more onto a single tiny chip.

With such impressive processing speed available, the MacBook Air can take on new extraordinarily intensive tasks like professional-quality editing, and action-packed gaming. But the 8-core CPU on M1 isn't just up to 3.5x faster than the previous generation — it also balances high-performance cores with efficiency cores that can still speed through everyday jobs while using just a tenth of the power.

8-core CPU

The 8-core CPU included with the MacBook Air is the highest-performing CPU Apple has ever built, by far. It combines four performance cores alongside four efficiency cores, that work together to tackle demanding multi-threaded tasks, resulting in a quantum leap in performance at a fraction of the power — and a significant boost to battery life.

8-core GPU

The GPU in the MacBook Air features the world's fastest integrated graphics in a personal computer. It's up to 5x faster when compared with the previous generation, and for the first time enables content creators to edit and seamlessly play back multiple streams of full-quality 4K video without dropping a frame.

Machine Learning

The dedicated 16-core Neural Engine in the M1 chip can execute up to a staggering 11 trillion operations per second, powering workflows you couldn't imagine before. Machine learning lets apps build and apply models based on massive amounts of data — to do things like identify friends and family in photos and videos, interpret natural language for dictation, and even analyse audio to recognise laughter, applause and more.

Touch ID

The latest MacBook Air introduces the ability to unlock your Mac, or make a purchase online, using just a fingertip. It's all performed via a small button in the upper-right corner of the keyboard. To protect the data about your fingerprint, the sensor which houses the reader is kept completely separate from your Mac. Called the T2 chip, it's a miniature computer in its own right, able to read your fingerprint, and also check the file system of your Mac at startup to ensure no one has tried to tamper with it. It's the most secure system of any notebook, so you can feel confident that your files and data are safe.

Keyboard and trackpad

The MacBook Air introduces Apple's third-generation butterfly keyboard, with keys that offer four times the stability of the previous keyboard, and a more responsive typing experience. In short, the keys move up and down a little more than previous butterfly keyboards, providing a more tactile experience when typing. The keyboard is also fully backlit, with individual LEDs behind each key, ensuring you can continue to type in low-light conditions, or even in the dark.

Perhaps the more obvious change to the lower part of the latest MacBook Air is its trackpad, which is now 20% larger than before. It supports force touch, so you can press harder to enable "3D Touch" features, like scrubbing quickly through a video; and it includes a haptic feedback motor, which can simulate clicks and subtle vibrations.

Audio

Laptops are perfect for watching videos on the couch, in bed, or at the back of a lecture hall, so it's important that they have great speakers which produce a rich sound. The acoustic engineering team at Apple have produced a set of speakers for the MacBook Air which are 25% louder than the earlier model, and which produce twice the bass, all within a svelte aluminium frame. The MacBook Air also features a three-microphone array, which ensures sound is crisp and clear in video calls or audio recordings, while also improving the experience of using Siri.

Ports

On the left side of the MacBook Air are two Thunderbolt 3 ports. Thunderbolt 3 features an ultra-high bandwidth rate while also supporting the USB-C industry standard, to create a versatile and powerful universal port. With support for up to 40Gb/s of throughput, a Thunderbolt port can transfer data, charge your MacBook Air, and provide video output, all at once.

Environmentally friendly

Producing consumer electronic devices can be harmful to the environment. Rare elements are used for battery components, while raw materials are often mined in third-world countries. The MacBook Air attempts to alleviate this problem by using recycled materials in as many components as possible. It starts with the aluminium - the metal which gives the MacBook Air its beautiful shine and feel, while also making it light and durable. In the past, Apple sourced its aluminium by mining high-purity ore; but for the MacBook Air, the company has designed an aluminium alloy which uses excess aluminium from other production processes, to ensure every part of the MacBook Air's enclosure is 100% recycled. This helps the carbon footprint of the MacBook Air to be roughly 50% less than the previous Air, while also making it the greenest Mac ever. Apple didn't stop there, because the tin used for the logic board is 100% recycled, while approximately 35% of the plastic used within the MacBook Air comes from recycled sources.

The Login Screen

How to select a user and login...

If your Macbook Air is turned off, hold down the **Power** button in the top-right corner of the keyboard, and after a moment it will power on. You'll then see the login screen:

An overview of the Login Screen:

When you reach the Login Screen, you may see a number of users displays across the centre of the screen. Alternatively, if your Mac is set to log you in automatically, then you may bypass this screen entirely and go straight to the desktop (see number one across the page to set this up or disable it).

1 Click on your username using the trackpad or a mouse. The login window will then appear. Enter your password, then either click **Log In** or press the **Enter** key on the keyboard. If you have forgotten your password, click on the Hint (**?**) button, and your Mac will display a password hint.

2 These shortcuts at the bottom of the screen enable you to turn off your Mac, restart it, or put it to sleep. In sleep mode, your MacBook will remain on but barely use any power. This is helpful if you know that you're going to use your Mac again in the next day or two

Customise the Login Screen

You can customise the Login Screen in several ways. For example, it's possible to automatically skip the Login Screen, hide the password hint, and enable a number of accessibility options. To do this, open the **System Preferences** app (you'll find it in the Dock at the bottom of the screen -- its icon looks like a set of cog wheels), click on **Users & Groups**, then click the **padlock** icon in the lower-left corner.

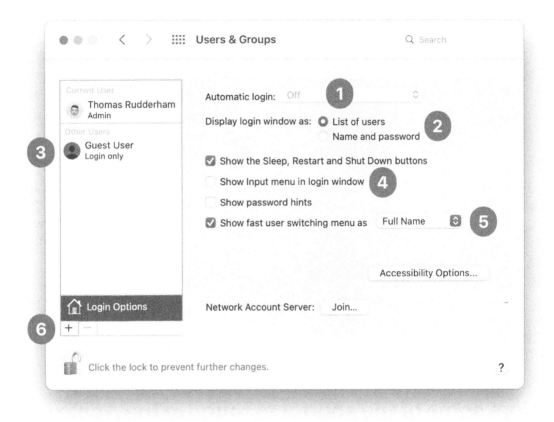

1. Automatic login will bypass the Login Screen entirely. This is helpful if you're the only one with access to your Mac, but can lead to security issues, so for your own privacy, it's best to leave Automatic login turned off.

2. With **List of users** selected, the Login Screen will display the names of each user on your Mac. When **Name and Password** is enabled, each user will have to manually enter their name and password -- which takes a little more time.

3. If you're the admin user for your Mac, then you can select another user to change their password and login items (apps which automatically open when they log in).

4. Tick **Show Input menu in login window** to let users choose the language they see after login.

5. This lets you quickly switch between users from the Login Screen. The dropdown menu enables you to choose how user accounts are displayed.

6. To add a new user account, click the **plus (+)** button. To remove an account, select it in the sidebar above, then click the **minus (-)** button.

17

Learn about Menus

Discover the basics of using menus on your Mac...

Unlike mobile operating systems such as iOS and Android, where icons and buttons are the primary methods of interacting with things, menus are an essential part of using your Mac. You'll need to use menus whenever you open or edit a file, interact with an app, or perform a task.

Turn on your Mac, look in the top-left corner and you'll see the Apple Menu. The Apple logo gives it away.

To use the Apple Menu, click on the **Apple** logo then choose an option. To close the menu, click anywhere outside the menu, or click on the Apple logo again.

Let's explore some of the shortcuts found in the Apple Menu:

About This Mac

Click on this option and you'll see a pop-up window displaying information about your Mac, including its software version, hardware configuration, software update options and available storage.

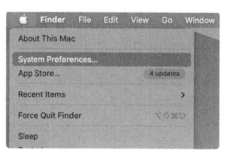

System Preferences & App Store

Quickly access the preferences app for your Mac, or visit the App Store where you can discover millions of apps.

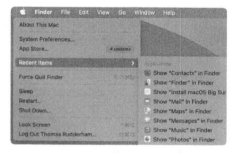

Recent Items

This menu option displays all of your recently opened apps, files, and folders.

Force Quit

If an app has crashed, click this shortcut in the Apple Menu to force-quit it.

Sleep, Restart and Shut Down

You can put your MacBook to sleep at any point by closing its lid, but you can also use this menu option in the Apple Menu. Notice the other two shortcuts for restarting your Mac or shutting it down fully.

Lock Screen

If you're stepping away from your Mac and want to quickly lock it -- without putting it to sleep -- click this option. When you return to the Mac you will be asked to re-enter your password.

Wondering what those icons at the top of the screen mean?

1 Get a detailed overview on your MacBook's current battery state. You can also get an idea of which apps are using significant battery charge.

2 Connect to Wi-Fi hotspots from this menu. You can also share your connection with other devices from this menu, or quickly jump to the Wi-Fi System Preferences panel.

3 If you have multiple user accounts set up on your Mac, then you can jump between them from this menu.

4 To search for anything on your Mac, such as files, folders, apps or settings, click the **search** icon in the menu.

5 Click this icon to open Control Centre, where you can manage basic settings with a single click. Turn over the page for more on this.

6 Click the **Siri** icon in the top-right corner to ask your Mac to perform a task. You can find out more about Siri later in this chapter.

7 See the date and time from this menu option. In the drop-down you'll also see an option for toggling between analog and digital formats.

Control Centre

Adjust basic settings with just a single click...

Tucked away in the menu bar are a helpful set of buttons for toggling settings and activating features. They include a slider for controlling the screen brightness, a button for enabling Wi-Fi, toggle Do Not Disturb, and more. To access these buttons at any time, click on the **Control Centre** button ( ) in the top-right corner of the menu.

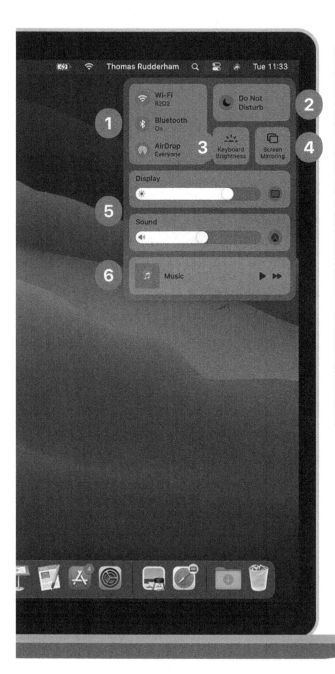

1 Toggle Wi-Fi, Bluetooth, or AirDrop on or off by clicking on their respective icons.

2 Click the **moon** icon to instantly toggle Do Not Disturb on or off. When enabled, you won't be interrupted by phone calls, messages, or notifications.

3 You can adjust the keyboard backlight brightness by clicking this button.

4 Click on the **Screen Mirroring** button to share your Mac's display with an Apple TV connected to the same Wi-Fi network.

5 Use these two sliders to adjust the display brightness or audio volume level. You can also click on the small buttons to the right of each to access additional settings.

6 Control music playback using this panel at the bottom of Control Centre.

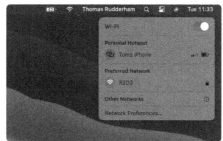

Access additional controls

When you move the mouse cursor over a control, a small arrow appears on the right. Click this arrow, and you can access additional controls. Here are a couple of examples...

Additional Wi-Fi settings

Click on the arrow to the right of the **Wi-Fi** button, and you'll see a toggle switch for disabling Wi-Fi, any additional Wi-Fi networks in the area, and a shortcut to Network Preferences.

Additional Display settings

Similarly, if you click on the Display arrow, you'll see toggle switches for Dark Mode, Night Shift, True Tone, plus shortcut links to Display and Sidecar Preferences.

Add additional modules to Control Centre

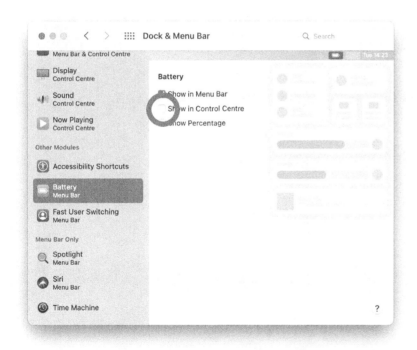

There are three additional modules that you can add to Control Centre:

- Accessibility Shortcuts
- Battery
- Fast User Switching

To add these modules, open **System Preferences**, then click **Dock & Menu Bar**. Scroll down the sidebar on the left, and you'll see shortcuts for each of these. To add them to Control Centre, simply click **Show in Control Centre**.

The Desktop

Learn how to use folders and organise your files...

Log into your Mac and the first place you visit is the Desktop. At the top of the Desktop is the Apple Menu, and at the bottom is the Dock, where all your favorite apps are located. Think of the Desktop as the home screen on your Mac. It's a place where you can leave folders, recent files and shortcuts to external drives. Or if you like to keep things tidy, nothing at all except a beautiful wallpaper.

Folders

Every file on your Mac is stored in something called a folder. Think of a folder like a storage box and you'll get the idea. Folders are great for organising things. You can have as many folders as you like on your Mac, and you can even have folders within folders. If you're a creative person, then you're likely to have a desktop covered in folders after a few weeks of owning a Mac.

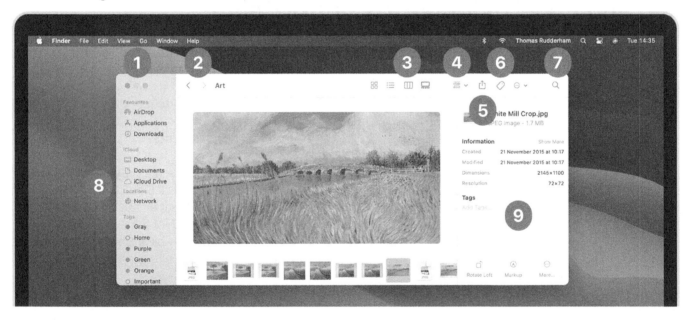

1 **Window controls.** See these small coloured gumdrops? You can use these to close, minimise/expand folders, apps, and windows.

2 **Navigation controls.** Go back or forward through your folders using these small chevron buttons.

3 **View options.** These buttons change the look of your folders. On the left is the grid view, followed by list, columns, and Gallery (seen here).

4 **Options.** Click the options button to sort a folder's contents by kind, date, size, and tag colour.

5 **Share.** The Share button lets you send a folder to others via Mail, Messages, AirDrop, and more.

6 **Tags.** Add a tag colour to a file or folder using this button.

7 **Search.** If you need to find a specific file or document, click this bar then type your query.

8 **Sidebar.** The left-hand sidebar acts a shortcut to various folders, drives, and devices.

9 **Information.** This panel on the right side of the window provides information about files, such as their size, date, and tags. When you select the Gallery view (as seen here), then you can also access shortcuts to common tasks such as editing photos and sharing files.

Resize a folder or window

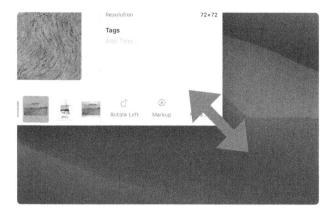

To make a folder bigger or smaller, hover the cursor over any corner of the folder, then click and drag it. You'll see the folder resize as you move the cursor around the screen. This also applies to app windows such as Safari or Mail.

Files

Whenever you work with an app or save something from the web, the data you have interacted with is saved as a file on your Mac. Files are basically pieces of data that are saved together in a single collection, and they come in a mindbogglingly vast number of formats, such as:

.jpg - an image.
.mov - a video file
.mp4 - another video file
.zip - a compressed file
.pages - a Pages file

Use Stacks to organise your desktop files

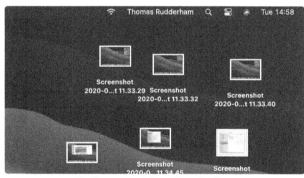

Before applying Stack view

By using the Stacks view you can automatically group all of the files on your desktop into sets. Let's say you have 10 jpg images, and 4 PDFs on your Desktop. When you use Stacks, those 10 images will be organised into a single stack, and there will be another stack containing the 4 PDFs. Here's how it works:

1 Click on **View** in the Finder menu, then choose **Use Stacks**.

2 You'll see all of your desktop files organise themselves into stacks.

3 To preview a stack of files, just hover the cursor over it, then perform the scroll gesture.

4 To open a stack, click on it. To close a stack, click away from it, or the close icon which has appeared.

After applying Stack view

Explore the Dock

Learn how to use and customise the Dock...

Think of the Dock as a shortcut to the Finder and all of your favorite applications, folders, and files. If you use something regularly, keep it in the Dock and it's never more than a click away.

When you first activate your Mac you'll see the Dock at the bottom of the screen, with the following items arranged from left to right:

- **The Finder**
- **Launchpad**
- **Default Apps**
- **System Preferences**

- **Currently-running apps**
- **Favorite files or folders**
- **The Trash**

The Dock is surprisingly flexible. You can resize it, rearrange items within it, snap it to the side of the screen, or even hide it when it's not needed. Here's how it looks on a brand new Mac:

Add an app to the Dock

If you regularly use an app then it's a good idea to add it to the Dock. Not only does that save time, but you'll also be able to see when the app is running on your Mac via a small dot underneath its icon.

To add an app from the Applications folder...

1. Open a Finder window, then click **Applications** in the sidebar.

2. Click and hold on an app, then drag it to the Dock.

3. Let go of the app while it's hovering over the Dock and it will drop into place.

If an app is already open on your Mac...

1. **Right-click** or **Control-click** on the app icon in the Dock.

2. Hover the cursor over **Options**.

3. Click on **Keep in Dock**.

Remove something from the Dock

If you want to remove something from the Dock, just click on the app, folder or file, then drag it off the Dock. You'll instantly see it disappear. You can also **right-click** or **Control-click** on the app icon, move the cursor over **Options**, and then un-select **Keep in Dock**.

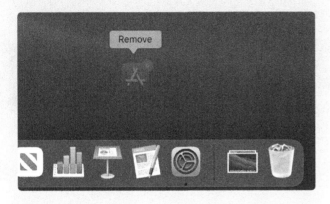

Rearrange items in the Dock

Most users place their most recently used apps on the left, while others group them by type. However you want to organise your Dock, it's easy to move apps around; simply click and hold on an app icon, then move it to where you want it to go.

Choose how folder contents appear via the Dock

Whenever you click on a folder in the Dock, your Mac reads its contents then displays them in a number of ways:

- If there are less than 15 items within the folder, you'll see a "Fan" arrangement appear, where the items are stacked one above the other.
- If there are 15 items or more within the folder, you'll see a fixed grid layout appear.

If you prefer one arrangement over the other, and want to set a default preference, **right-click** on the folder within the Dock, look for "**View content as**" in the pop-up window and choose your preference. You'll also see a third option called List, which displays the folder contents as a (you guessed it) list.

Make the Dock bigger or smaller

By default the Dock is pretty big and takes up a considerable amount of space at the bottom of the screen. By making it smaller not only do you gain more vertical space for apps and content, but you can also add more apps, folders, and shortcuts to the Dock. Here's how to adjust the size of the Dock to your liking:

A tiny Dock...

A massive Dock...

1. Open the **System Preferences** app and click **Dock**.

2. Drag the **Size** slider left or right to increase or decrease the size of the Dock. You'll see it change in real-time as you move the slider.

3. Alternatively, if you hover the mouse over the faint black line on the Dock which separates apps from folders and files, you'll see the cursor turn to a double-headed arrow. By clicking and dragging left or right, you can adjust the size of the Dock without going into System Preferences.

Make Dock items magnify as you scroll over them

The Dock has a great visual animation effect which 'zooms' icons into view as you move the cursor over them. It's completely unnecessary, but looks great, while adding some visual charm. Here's how to enable and tweak the effect:

1. Open the **System Preferences** app and click **Dock & Menu Bar**.

2. Tick the **Magnification** box.

3. Drag the **Magnification** slider left or right to adjust the effect.

4. Test the effect by hovering the cursor over an app in the Dock.

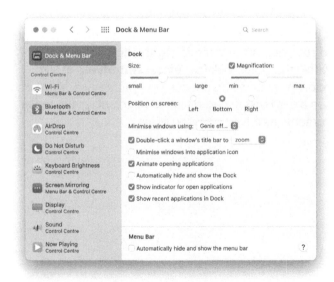

Snap the Dock to the side of your screen

As you might have already noticed, your MacBook display is wider than it is tall. This is great for watching movies or browsing through photos, but can restrict your view when browsing web pages or writing long documents.

If you want to gain a little bit of extra vertical space, then snapping the Dock to the left or right is a good idea. To do this:

1 Open the **System Preferences** app and click **Dock**.

2 Look towards the middle of the next panel and you'll see options for placing the Dock on the **Left, Bottom** (default) or **Right**. Click on an option to see how it looks and feels.

Add spaces to your Dock

If you're a professional user, chances are you have a *lot* of apps, folders, and files in your Dock. To help organise your Dock, it's possible to add spaces between apps or folders to help you categorise them. It's a little fiddly and requires using the Terminal app, so this is only recommended for those who feel confident using their Mac. Here's how:

1 Open the **Terminal** app.

2 Enter the following text, as many times as you wish, to add spaces: **defaults write com.apple.dock persistent-apps -array-add '{"tile-type"="spacer-tile";}'**

3 Force restart the Dock to make the spaces appear by entering this into Terminal: **killall Dock**

You can move spaces around by clicking and dragging them, and you can remove them by dragging them off the Dock.

Touch ID

Set up Touch ID so you can unlock your MacBook using your fingerprint...

TouchID is pretty amazing. It works by recognising your fingerprint when you place it on the small black square in the top-right corner of the keyboard. Once enabled, you can unlock your Mac with your fingerprint, or purchase an item over the internet using Apple Pay.

It's worth noting that your Mac and its operating system can never access your fingerprint record. Instead, it's stored in a secure part of the Touch Bar hardware; and it never leaves the Touch Bar, so when you place your fingerprint on the sensor, either a yes or no signal is sent to the operating system.

Keeping your personal data safe is one of Apple's most pressing priorities, so here's what the company does to ensure your fingerprint never leaves your MacBook:

- The MacBook and its operating system can never access your fingerprint. Instead, it's stored in a secure part of the TouchID bar. Only the fingerprint sensor beneath the Touch ID button can access your print, and it only sends a yes or no signal to macOS when you place your fingertip on the sensor.

- Your fingerprint never leaves the physical device. That means it can't be accessed by the NSA, hackers or anyone else.

How to set up Touch ID

1 Your Mac will ask you to set up Touch ID when you activate it for the very first time. If you skipped that step, just click on the **Apple** menu button on the top-left of your screen, click **System Preferences**, select **Touch ID**, then click **Add a fingerprint**.

2 Place your thumb or finger on the Touch ID sensor. You'll see a graphic of a fingerprint appear and slowly start to turn red. Keep placing your fingerprint on the sensor until the graphic has completely turned red. The next step is to capture the surrounding areas of your fingerprint. This is to ensure the sensor can read your finger when it's tilted or leaning to one side. The most efficient way to complete this process is to place your finger on the sensor at an angle, lift it, roll your finger slightly then place it down again.

3 Repeat this process until you've rolled your finger all the way around and the graphic has turned red.

Next, click the **Continue** button. Your fingerprint has been added and can now be used.

Fingerprint options

Now that you've added a fingerprint, you'll notice checkbox buttons which enable you to unlock your MacBook, purchase items using Apple Pay, and enter your password. Tick any of the options you wish to use.

Delete or rename a fingerprint

To remove a fingerprint, simply hover the cursor over the fingerprint, then click the small **X** button which appears. You can also name fingerprints by clicking on the finger name, then typing a replacement into the text field.

Connect to a Wi-Fi network

Easily connect to home, office, or public Wi-Fi networks...

Connecting to a Wi-Fi network is one of those really basic tasks that we all must do from time to time. Perhaps you're visiting a friend and would like to hook up to their internet connection, or you might be sat in a coffee shop that offers free Wi-Fi.

When you first activate your Mac, you'll be asked to connect to the nearest Wi-Fi network and walked through that process. If you skipped that step, or need a reminder, then here's how to connect to a Wi-Fi network on your Mac:

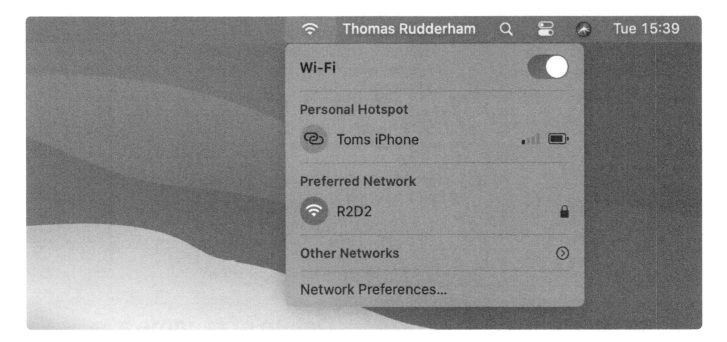

1. Begin by clicking on the **Wi-Fi** icon (🛜) in the menu at the top of the screen.

2. A list of Wi-Fi connections will appear in the drop-down menu.

3. Select a wireless network. You might see a small padlock icon next to some of the networks, that means they require a password. If so the password entry screen will appear, just enter the password when prompted, then click **Join**. If you've entered it successfully, then your Mac will automatically join the network.

Configure a preferred Wi-Fi network

If you want to explore the Wi-Fi settings on your Mac or make some changes, then here's how it's done:

1 Open **System Preferences**, then click on **Network**.

2 Click the **Advanced** button in the lower-right corner.

3 You'll see a list of all the Wi-Fi connections you Mac has connected to, in order of preference. If there are two available locally, then your Mac will always connect to the one at the top.

4 If you want to change this order, simply **click and drag** the connections up and down.

5 To remove a network connection, click on it, then click the minus button below the list.

Public networks

If the network doesn't require a password then you can simply click on the Wi-Fi network name and immediately connect to the web. Note however, that sometimes networks require you to enter personal details via the Safari app before you can freely browse the web. You'll probably come across this situation in coffee shops and airports. Hotels might also request you to enter your hotel room number and a password, the latter of which is typically available from the reception.

Problems with WiFi

In case you encounter some issues with the Wi-Fi, here are a few things you can try to remedy it:

1 Make sure the router is switch on and is connected. You can usually do this by looking at the router. If it has green lights flashing, then everything is fine. If there seems to be a problem, try disconnecting the power, reconnecting it then wait a few minutes.

2 Check the Wi-Fi signal on your Mac. You'll see it in the menu bar in the upper right corner. If the signal is strong, then you'll see four bars. If you see less, try moving your Mac closer to the router. Thick walls can also block the connection.

Discover apps

There's a whole world of apps available for your Mac...

Without any third-party apps, your Mac would basically be a glorified web browser. Thankfully, there are literally millions of apps available for you to install and enjoy, including photo editors, games, music production tools and more.

Before we get to third-party apps, let's explore the ones which are already installed on your Mac...

Launchpad

Every application and utility is stored in an area of the Desktop called Launchpad. It's a bit like the Home screen on an iPhone or iPad, enabling you to browse your apps, arrange them into folders and (if installed from the App Store), and even delete them.

The easiest way to access Launchpad at any time is to click the **Launchpad** icon in the Dock. It looks like a small collection coloured cubes, and by default, it's located on the left-side of the Dock.

If you've removed Launchpad from the Dock then you can also access it by pinching closed your thumb and three fingers on the trackpad.

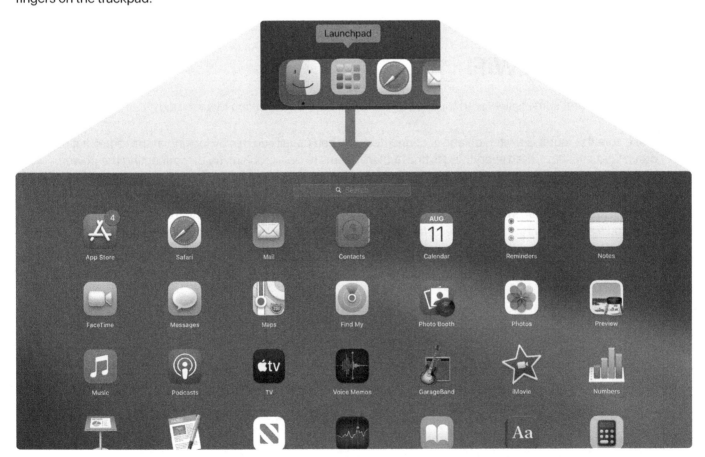

Add an app to Launchpad

Any app you download from the App Store is automatically added to Launchpad. Similarly, any apps added to the Applications folder on your Mac. You can find a shortcut to the Applications folder in the sidebar of a folder window.

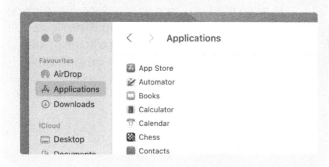

Search for an app

If you have a wealth of apps installed on your Mac and want to quickly find the right one, just start typing its name when you're viewing Launchpad and you'll automatically see it appear.

Organise your apps

Moving apps around Launchpad or re-organising them into folders is easy:

Re-arrange apps: Drag an app to a new location using the trackpad or mouse.

Create a folder: Simply drag an app on top of another.

Rename a folder: When viewing a folder click its name then enter a new one.

Delete an app from Launchpad

To delete an app, simply **click and hold** on the app icon, then when it starts to jiggle click the **X** icon.

If you don't see the X icon appear, then the app is either required to be installed on your Mac, or the app was installed outside of the App Store. If it's the latter and you still want to delete the app:

1 Go to the Finder, click **Go** in the menu bar then choose **Applications**.

2 Drag the app icon or folder to the **Trash** icon in the Dock.

3 Alternatively, right-click on the app or app folder then choose **Move to Trash**.

Check out the App Store

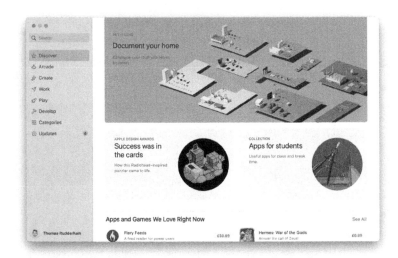

As you might have guessed, the App Store is the best place to find new and exciting apps for your Mac. It's updated constantly with the latest apps, updates and games, and because every app is approved by Apple, you don't have to worry about spam or hidden viruses.

To open the App Store on your Mac, just click on **Launchpad**, then click the **App Store** icon. You can also click on the **Apple** logo in the menu at the top of the screen, then choose **App Store**.

Install an app

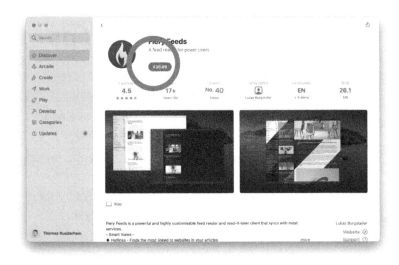

When you're ready to install an app, click on its **price**, then the blue **Buy App** button. If the app is free, it works in the same way: just click **Get**, then the blue **Install App** button.

View your app purchases or redeem a promo code

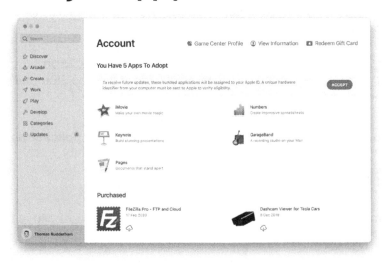

When viewing the App Store on your Mac, click on your **profile** photo in the bottom-left corner. On the following screen you'll see every app purchase you've ever made, alongside free apps you've downloaded. To re-download an app click on the **cloud** icon.

From this screen you can also redeem a promo code. Just click the **Redeem Gift Card** button in the top-right corner then follow the on-screen prompts to enter the gift card's code.

How to install apps from the web

So you've downloaded an app from the web. What next? The process of unpacking and installing a third-party application from the internet is slightly more complicated than using the App Store. Here's how it works:

1 Everything you download is saved to the Downloads folder. You can find this towards the right-side of the Dock. Alternatively, if you're on the Desktop click **Go** in the Finder menu then choose **Downloads**.

2 Look for the application you've downloaded. If it's a zip file just double-click to unzip it.

3 Double-click on the unzipped file. If you get an error message that says "*This program can't be opened because it wasn't downloaded from the Mac App Store*," don't worry, all you need to do is right-click on the file and select **Open**.

4 A folder will be mounted on the Desktop which contains an installation file. Double-click this file then follow the on-screen instructions to install the app.

5 Once the installation process has completed, close it then eject the mounted folder by either dragging it to the **Trash** or by clicking the **eject** button in the Finder window sidebar.

Talk to Siri

Take command of your very own assistant...

Imagine Siri as your very own personal assistant. He (or she depending on your country of origin), can make FaceTime calls for you, dictate emails and messages, make a restaurant reservation, remind you to do things, tell you about movies, make jokes, and much more.

Siri isn't perfect, however. It can't remember interactions from the past, it relies on hearing your voice in a clear manner, and it needs a connection to the internet to work. If you're aware of these limitations and don't mind the odd false request, then Siri can save time and even be a little fun to use.

There are three ways to enable Siri:

1 Click the **Siri** icon in the Dock.

2 Press the **Siri** button in the top-right corner of the Touch bar.

3 Click the **Siri** icon in the top-right corner of the Apple Menu (⚫).

Speak to Siri

Next, say out loud, "*What's the weather like today?*" Siri will automatically look for a weather report then tell you what it's going to be like. It's that simple to use Siri.

Enable 'Type to Siri'

Sometimes it's not appropriate, or possible, to talk to Siri, so your Mac offers the option to type to Siri instead. To enable Type to Siri:

1 Click on the **Apple** menu, then **System Preferences.**

2 Click on the **Accessibility** option.

3 Scroll down the sidebar and choose **Siri**.

4 Click the **Enable Type to Siri** checkbox. Now, when you activate Siri, you'll see a text box. Type a query and press Enter on your keyboard to use it.

Activate Siri with a keyboard shortcut

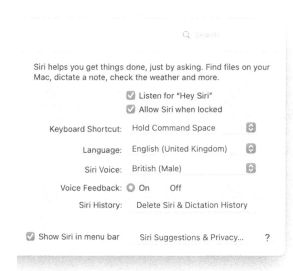

Siri helps you get things done, just by asking. Find files on your Mac, dictate a note, check the weather and more.

☑ Listen for "Hey Siri"
☑ Allow Siri when locked

Keyboard Shortcut: Hold Command Space

Language: English (United Kingdom)

Siri Voice: British (Male)

Voice Feedback: ● On   Off

Siri History: Delete Siri & Dictation History

☑ Show Siri in menu bar   Siri Suggestions & Privacy...   ?

To activate Siri using the keyboard, press **Command-Space**. To use a different keyboard shortcut:

1 Click on the **Apple** menu then **System Preferences**.

2 Click on the **Siri** option.

3 Under **Keyboard Shortcut**, use the drop-down menu to select another option. You can choose from Command-Space (default), Option-Space, Function-Space, or you can create your own keyboard shortcut.

Things you can ask Siri...

"Play something by Monsters and Men"

"Remind me to call Michael at 7."

"Send a message to Dave"

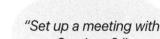
"Set up a meeting with Sarah at 9."

"Email Chris to say I'm running late."

"Show me movies directed by Steven Spielberg"

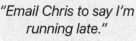
"Find the files I worked on yesterday."

"Put the Mac to sleep."

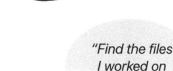

Use AirDrop to share files

Send photos or files to friends nearby...

Whenever you need to share a file with another Mac, iPhone, or iPad, AirDrop is the answer. It works by sending files to other Apple devices within a 30 feet radius. You can send anything you like, from photos, videos, or files; and the devices don't need to share the same Apple ID, so you can share files with nearly anyone, so long as they have an Apple device.

Send a file

To share a file from the Finder, click on **Go** in the menu at the top of the screen, then choose **AirDrop**. You can also use the keyboard shortcut **Shift-Command-R**.

You'll see the AirDrop Finder window open. If any devices are within reach, they will appear here. To send a file, simply drag and drop it onto the device. If the device has a different Apple ID, then the owner will need to approve the transfer; otherwise the file will automatically be transferred and opened.

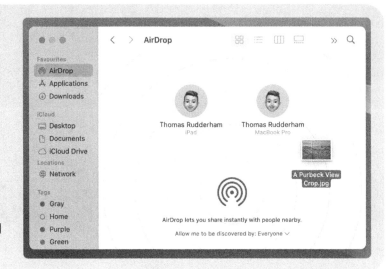

Share a file using an app

If you want to share something in an app, like a webpage in Safari, or a document in Pages, click the **Share** icon (it looks like a square with an arrow pointing up), then choose **AirDrop** from the menu. You can then use the AirDrop window to share the file.

Control who can see your Mac

If you're in a public space and don't want others to see your Mac in AirDrop, open the AirDrop panel via the Finder, click on the blue piece of text that says "*Allow me to be discovered by: Everyone*", and choose from either people in your contacts list, or no-one.

If you can't see someone...

If they are using an iPad or iPhone, ask them to open the AirDrop panel in Control Centre, then enable AirDrop.

If they are using a Mac, ask them to open the AirDrop window via the Finder and they should appear.

Use AirPlay to stream content

Send video and music to your TV, or even your Mac's entire screen...

With AirPlay you can wirelessly stream content to an Apple TV, or play music over AirPlay speakers such as HomePod. All you need to do is connect your Mac to the same Wi-Fi connection shared with your AirPlay devices; there are no complicated configurations to set up, all the hard work is done for you.

What you can stream to an AirPlay device:

- Music and Beats 1 Radio

What you can stream to an Apple TV:

- Movies and videos
- Music and Beats 1 Radio
- Photos and slideshows
- Your entire Mac display

Stream content to your Apple TV

Whenever you're listening to music or watching a video and want to stream it to an Apple TV, click the **AirPlay** button, then select your Apple TV. It looks like a square with an up arrow in the lower-middle.

If you don't see the AirPlay button, chances are the app or website doesn't support AirPlay streaming.

Mirror your display to an Apple TV

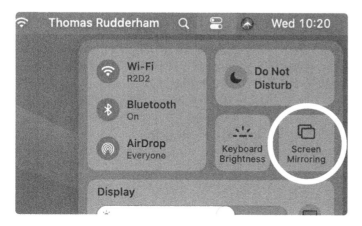

If you want to show your Mac's display on an Apple TV, click the **Control Panel** button in the top-right corner of the menu menu, choose **Screen Mirroring**, then select the Apple TV.

When AirPlay is active, the menu bar will turn blue to let you know. If the image doesn't fit the screen properly when you mirror the screen, you can adjust the desktop size by clicking the **AirPlay** icon, then choosing an option under **Match Desktop Size To.**

How to use Spotlight

Learn how to find files, hide folders and more...

Think of Spotlight as Google, but instead of searching the web you're searching your Mac. Using Spotlight you can pretty much search for anything you can think of. Files, emails, apps, music tracks, contacts, and even information within documents.

That's not all, because Spotlight does a pretty good job of replacing Google too, so you can use it to search for Wikipedia information, flight times, sports results, and more.

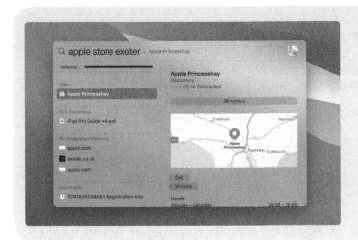

How to access Spotlight

It's easy, just click on the **magnifying glass** icon in the menu bar at the top of the screen, then start typing a search query.

You can search for things like "apple store" or "emails from Sam". You can also open Spotlight using the keyboard shortcut: command-space.

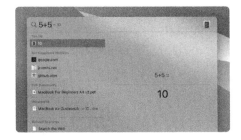

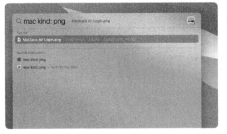

Calculations and conversions

To calculate something, type "5+5" into Spotlight.

To convert something, type "20 feet to metres".

To see the definition of a word, type it then click the result in the Definition section.

Search for a specific type of file

To search for a specific type of file, type "kind:" then the type of file. For example, you can search for "kind:jpg", "kind:folder", or "kind:video".

See a file's location on your Mac

To see the location of a file on your Mac, click on the search result, then press and hold the **Command** key. The file's location will then appear in the bottom of the Spotlight window. To open the location, press **Command-R**.

How to customise search results

If Spotlight doesn't find what you're looking for, or if you want to limit where it should and shouldn't be searching, then here's how you can customise search results:

1 Click on the **Apple** menu button on the top-left of your screen.

2 Click **System Preferences**.

3 Click on **Spotlight**.

4 Un-tick items to hide them from Spotlight results, or tick them to show them.

Hide a folder from Spotlight

If you want to hide a folder from Spotlight results:

1 Open **System Preferences** and click on **Spotlight**.

2 Click the **Privacy** tab.

3 Click the **plus** icon in the lower-left corner, then select a folder. It will now be hidden from Spotlight results.

4 You can also drag a folder to this panel to add it.

Notifications and Widgets

Discover how to manage notifications and widgets...

Notifications on your Mac let you know about updates, new messages, and other activities going within apps and the operating system. There are typically two ways a notification might appear on your Mac:

● **Notification alerts**
Whenever your Mac or an app wants to let you know about something, a small notification window will appear in the top-right corner of the screen. You might see that an update is available, or it could be a new message from a friend.

● **App badges**
If you see a small red dot above the app icon in your Dock, then the app is letting you know that a new message or update is awaiting.

You can also see all of your notifications in one place: Notification Centre. From here you can see all your app notifications, missed calls, calendar events, and messages. You can also access widgets from here. These are small panels of information, such as the latest stocks or weather.

How to access Notification Centre

To open Notification Centre at any time, click the **date and time** in the very top-right corner of your screen. You can also use a two-finger swipe from right to left, starting at the right edge of your Mac's trackpad.

When you open Notification Centre, you'll see a number of widgets running down the side of the screen. These are designed to quickly provide information at a glance, but you can click on each of them to open the corresponding app. For example if you click on a message notification, it will take you to the corresponding app. For example, if you click on a Message notification, then the Messages app will open.

Add or remove widgets

When you open Notification Centre you'll see a small number of widgets, including the weather and stocks. To add more widgets, remove widgets or rearrange them:

- **To remove widgets:** Click **Edit Widgets** at the bottom of the screen, then click on the **minus** button which appears over the widget.

- **To add widgets:** Move the cursor over the widget you'd like to add, then click the **green plus** button which appears

- **To rearrange widgets:** Click and hold on a widget, then drag it to its new location.

Customise notification alerts

If an app is constantly sending your alerts, or you want to customise how alerts appear on your Mac, then here's how you can disable or edit them:

1. Open **System Preferences,** then choose **Notifications**.

2. Select an app from the sidebar. You can then choose from banner alerts, small alerts or none.

3. You can also disable badge icons and sounds for each app.

Reply to a message without using the Messages app

If a message notification appears while you're using your Mac, click the **Show More** button and you'll be able to send a reply without going into the Messages app.

Accounts, emails, and passwords

Learn how to add your email account, calendar events, and passwords...

As you use your Mac to do day-to-day things, such as checking emails, adding calendar events, or logging into websites, then you're going to start accumulating login details, accounts, and passwords. On this page you'll learn the basics of adding accounts and personal details. Most of it happens automatically, and once you've added an account you'll be able to start emailing friends and family, check your calendar for events, plus much more.

Add your email account

Start by opening the **System Preferences** app, then click on **Internet Accounts**.

Select your email provider. If your email address ends with "gmail.com", then click on Google. If it ends with "hotmail.com", select the Outlook option. You get the idea.

Your Mac will ask for the username and password associated with your email account. Simply enter these and click **Next**.

Some providers, such as Gmail, will require that you enter your details using the Safari browser.

Your Mac will verify your mail account details. Once the process has completed you can choose whether you wish to sync mail, contacts and notes.

Add calendar events you've saved to Gmail, Outlook, or a personal account

If you've ever used a Gmail or Outlook account to add calendar events, then your Mac can automatically load these from the internet and add them to the Calendar app. Similarly, when you add a new event or modify an existing one, your Mac will sync the changes to your account on the internet. This means if you log into your account using a web browser or another computer, all the changes you made on your Mac will appear there too.

If you've already added your Apple, Gmail, Outlook, or Yahoo account...

1. Start by opening the **System Preferences** app, then click on **Internet Accounts**.

2. Click on your account.

3. On the following screen, tick the **Calendars** button.

If you're adding a new account...

1. Start by opening the **System Preferences** app, then click on **Internet Accounts**.

2. Click on your email provider, or click the **plus** button in the bottom-left corner.

3. Your Mac will ask for the username and password associated with your email account. Simply enter these and click **Next**.

4. Your Mac will verify your mail account details. Once the process has completed you can choose whether you wish to sync mail, contacts, calendar and notes.

Look for a password or username

Whenever you log into a website and enter a username, email address, or password, your Mac will ask if you would like to save these details on the device. If you agree, the next time you go back to the website and try to log in, your Mac will automatically offer to enter your details. It's a great time-saving feature, and it also means you don't have to remember every single password you've ever entered.

Sometimes you might need to take a look at these passwords and login details. Perhaps you're using someone else's computer and can't remember your password, or maybe you've accidentally saved multiple login details for a site and want to tidy them up. Here's how you can access every password and account saved on your Mac in a few steps...

1. Open **Safari** on your Mac, click on **Safari** in the Apple menu at the top of the screen, then click **Preferences**.

2. Click on the **Passwords** tab, then enter your Apple ID password or use your fingerprint to unlock the panel.

3. You'll then see a list of every website you've ever logged into.

4. You can search for a website, username, email address, or password, by using the search field at the top of the panel.

5. You can also click on individual accounts to see the details you've saved.

6. To delete a set of details, select it then click the **Remove** button at the bottom of the panel.

How to cut, copy, and paste

Discover how to copy something then paste it somewhere else...

Copying and pasting is a great way to move text or content from one app to another. For example, you could copy your address from Contacts then paste it into Safari, or copy a photo from the internet and then paste it into an email. Here's how it works...

Copy text

Find a source of text on your Mac, perhaps your phone number in Contacts. **Right-click** on the number, then choose **Copy** from the pop-up menu. You can also press **Command-C** on the keyboard.

Paste text

Next, close Contacts and open the Notes app. Create a new note or select an existing one, **right-click** within the note and choose **Paste**. You can also press **Command-V** on the keyboard.

Copy images

To copy an image from the internet, open Safari, find an image on any website, **right-click** on it and choose **Copy Image**. You can now paste this image into a new email, message, note, or graphic-based app.

Copy and paste between Mac and iPhone or iPad

Copying and pasting is a great way to quickly move content from one app to another. With just a few clicks it's possible to copy text in Notes then paste it into Safari, or copy an image from the web and paste it into an email. However, it's also possible to copy content from one Apple device to another. For example, let's copy an website address from Safari on your Mac, then paste it into Safari on an iPhone.

1 Start by opening Safari on your Mac, then go to www.apple.com. Next, **right-click** on the website address bar at the top of the browser window and choose **Copy** in the pop-up window.

2 Next, using your iPhone, open the Safari app. Tap on the address field at the top of the screen, clear it by tapping the small **x** button, then **double-tap** on the address bar. In the small pop-up field, tap **Paste** and you'll see www.apple.com instantly appear in the address field.

This process of copying content from one device to another works seamlessly on iPhone, iPad and the Mac, but with one caveat: you need to be signed into the same Apple ID on every device.

Use Handoff to work between devices

Start something on your Mac, then continue it on your iPad or iPhone...

Most people won't have heard about Handoff. It's a rather clever feature which lets you start something on your Mac, then continue it on an iPad or iPhone.

Take writing an email for example. You might begin to compose an email on your Mac, then later finish it on the go using your iPhone; or maybe you start reading a web page on your Mac, then continue it on an iPad. Here's how it works:

Turn Handoff on

To enable Handoff on your Mac, open **System Preferences**, click **General**, then ensure **Allow Handoff between this Mac and your iCloud devices** is ticked.

To enable Handoff on your iPhone and iPad, go to **Settings** > **General** > **Handoff & Suggested Apps**, then toggle the **Handoff** switch on.

Jump from iPhone to Mac

It's easy to swap tasks between an iPhone and Mac. Take reading a web page for example. When you open a web page on your iPhone, a Safari icon will appear on the left-side of the Dock on the Mac.

Just click on this icon to open the same webpage on your Mac. This same process goes for composing Notes, Emails and Messages, or adding Calendar and Contact entries.

Jump from iPhone to iPad

If you'd like to continue a task on your iPad, begin writing, adding or reading content on your iPhone, then turn on your iPad. On the Lock Screen you'll see the relevant app icon in the bottom left corner of the screen. Just tap or swipe it upwards to jump to the same content on your iPad. If the icon doesn't appear, ensure Bluetooth is turned on by swiping upwards to reveal Control Centre, then tap the **Bluetooth** icon.

Requirements

Handoff requires every device to have Bluetooth enabled, and they all need to be approximately 30 feet or less from each other.

Use Apple Pay to buy things

Leave your wallet in the drawer...

Apple Pay is pretty remarkable. You can use it to pay for apps and music with your Mac, or buy items online without entering your credit card details.

What is Apple Pay?

It's a way of paying for things by holding your iPhone or Apple Watch near a contactless payment terminal. On a Mac, you can use it online to pay for goods, or within apps when you see the Apple Pay logo, which looks like this:

Enable Apple Pay on your Mac

1 Open the **System Preferences** app, click on **Wallet & Apple Pay**, then follow the steps to add a card. If you're trying to add a card which already exists within your Apple ID account, then you'll only need to enter its security code.

2 Click **Next** and your bank will authorise and add your card. If your bank needs more details you can add these later via **System Preferences** > **Wallet & Apple Pay**.

Use Apple Pay online

If a website supports Apple Pay, you'll see a button at the checkout with the words "Check Out with Apple Pay". Click this button to make the purchase immediately using your Apple Pay account.

Use Apple Pay in an app

If you're using an app and see the Apple Pay logo, you might need to toggle a setting that enables Apple Pay first, the app will let you know. Once enabled, click the **Apple Pay** button, ensure all the details are correct, then use Touch ID to confirm your identity.

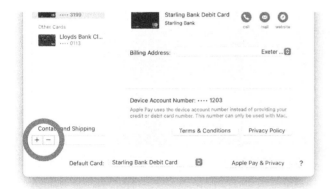

Add or remove credit cards

1 Open the **System Preferences** app, then select **Wallet & Apple Pay.**

2 To add a new credit card, click the **plus (+)** button below the sidebar.

3 To remove a card, select it using the sidebar then click the **minus (-)** button below the sidebar.

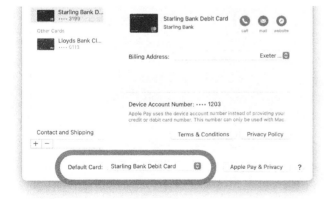

Choose which card to use

The credit card linked to your Apple ID will automatically be the default card used for Apple Pay. If you would like to use a different card:

1 Open the **System Preferences** app, then select **Wallet & Apple Pay.**

2 Use the **Default Card** drop-down at the bottom of the panel to select another credit card.

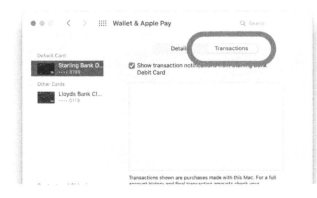

See your recent transactions

Every time you use Apple Pay the last few transactions will be stored as virtual receipts on your Mac. To see these:

1 Open the **System Preferences** app, then select **Wallet & Apple Pay.**

2 Click the **Transactions** tab at the top of the panel.

Magic Mouse gestures

There's more to the Magic Mouse than just clicking...

A Magic Mouse doesn't come included with the MacBook, but it's a worthwhile purchase for anyone who plans to use their Mac for productive purposes. That's because a mouse is far more accurate than a trackpad for manipulating small interface elements such as buttons and per-pixel-sized objects.

It's also packed with clever technologies, including a large touch-sensitive area on the top, which enables gestures to be used to scroll, zoom, and navigate through content:

Secondary Click

Press firmly on the right side of the Magic Mouse and you'll perform a secondary click, also known as a right-click in some circles. This action enables you to access shortcut menus or secondary features.

If the secondary click feature is disabled on your Mac, open the **System Preferences** app, select **Mouse**, then toggle **Secondary Click** on.

Scroll

To scroll through web pages or documents, slowly swipe your finger up and down the middle of the mouse. By flicking your finger you can scroll quicker.

If you don't like the direction in which scroll works, then you can flip it vertically. To do this open the **System Preferences** app, select **Mouse**, then toggle **Scroll Direction: Natural** off.

Swipe between pages

If you're using Safari and want to go back a page, just swipe your finger across the top of the mouse from left to right. You can also go forward by swiping right to left.

This isn't turned on by default, so to enable this feature open the **System Preferences** app, select **Mouse**, click the **More Gestures** tab, then enable **Swipe between pages**.

Swipe between full-screen apps

If you prefer to run your apps in full-screen mode, then you can quickly jump from one app to another by swiping left or right across the mouse with two fingers.

Quickly access Mission Control

Double-tap on the mouse with two fingers and you'll jump into Mission Control, which displays all your apps and windows on one screen.

Enable Smart Zoom

Smart Zoom lets you zoom into content by tapping twice on the top of the mouse. To enable this feature open the **System Preferences** app, select **Mouse**, then toggle **Smart Zoom** on.

Adjust the tracking speed

If you find that the mouse cursor moves too quickly or slowly, then it's possible to adjust the tracking speed to something more comfortable. To do this:

1 Open the **System Preferences** app, then select **Mouse.**

2 Look for the Tracking Speed slider, in the bottom half of the panel.

3 Drag the small slider button right to increase the tracking speed, or left to slow it down.

Mouse settings

Scroll and click how you like...

You might think of the mouse as something that's uncompromising; something that hasn't changed in decades, with no options for personalisation. As it turns out, the Magic Mouse is quite the opposite. It has a touch sensor on the top panel, enabling you to perform basic gestures, while its scrolling speed and direction can be tweaked to suit your preferences.

Make the mouse cursor bigger

If you often find yourself struggling to find the mouse cursor, then it's possible to make it larger using an accessibility setting. Here's how:

1 Open the **System Preferences** app, then select **Accessibility**.

2 Select **Display** in the sidebar, click the **Cursor** tab, then use the **Cursor size** slider to increase the size of the mouse cursor.

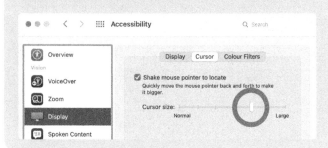

Change the scroll direction

By default, when you scroll a page using the mouse, it moves in the opposite direction, so to move the page down, you scroll up. If you find this confusing, and would like to scroll the "natural" way, then:

1 Open the **System Preferences** app, then choose **Mouse**.

2 Tick the box for **Scrolling direction: Natural** to make the mouse scroll the same direction as your finger.

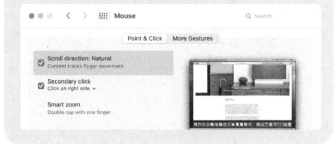

Use Smart Zoom

By tapping the top of your mouse twice it's possible to zoom into photos and web pages. If this isn't enabled on your Mac, head over to **System Preferences**, select **Mouse** then click the **Smart Zoom** checkbox.

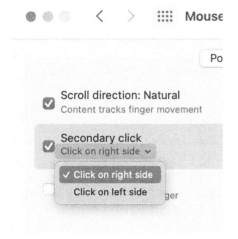

Enable secondary click on your Mouse

If you're planning to use your Mac for productive work, or want to really make the most out of it, then it's a good idea to enable secondary click functionality. It works how you might imagine, assigning the right side of your mouse as a secondary (or right) click. Once activated, you can access secondary functions across the entirety of your Mac, enabling you to perform shortcuts and tasks that are otherwise hidden away in menus.

To enable right-click functionality, open the **System Preferences** app, choose **Mouse**, then enable the **Secondary click** option. If you would like to assign the left-side of the mouse as the secondary click option, instead of the right side, click the small drop-down arrow beneath the Secondary click option, then choose **Click on left side**.

Enable secondary click on your Mouse

If you're a pro with the mouse, then you probably double-click on things really fast. If you're a little slower, or struggle with physically pressing the mouse down, then it's possible to slow the wait time between clicks - even down to four seconds. Here's how:

1. Open the **System Preferences** app, then select **Accessibility**.

2. Select **Pointer Control** in the sidebar.

3. Drag the **Double-click speed** slider to the right to increase how quickly you would like to double-click, or to the left to decrease it.

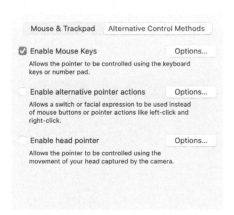

Use an external keyboard to move the mouse cursor

If you have trouble controlling the mouse then it's possible to use the number pad on an external keyboard to move the cursor and select things. To do this:

1. Open the **System Preferences** app, then select **Accessibility**.

2. Select **Pointer Control** in the sidebar.

3. Click the **Alternative Control Methods** tab.

4. Click **Enable Mouse Keys**.

Now, when you press the number keys on your keyboard, the cursor will move. 8 moves it upwards, 6 moves it right, 2 moves it down, and 4 moves it left. To click the cursor, press 5. You can also use 7, 9, 1, and 3, to move the cursor diagonally.

Trackpad gestures

Find out how to scroll, zoom and more...

It might not be obvious, but the large trackpad beneath the keyboard of your MacBook supports Multi-Touch gestures; just like the iPhone and iPad.

Admittedly, it's not quite as intuitive as a touchscreen device, because there's no direct contact between your fingertip and the screen, but nevertheless, with a little practice, you'll soon be swiping between pages, zooming into photos, and scrolling through lists with ease.

The trick to using the trackpad is to practice with both fingers whenever you get the chance. You'll soon learn which gestures use one finger, which use two, and which even use three. You'll also learn how to move your fingers gently and smoothly across the trackpad.

Enable Multi-Touch gestures

Basic gestures are already enabled when you activate your Mac, but some of the advanced gestures, such as Look up data detectors, need to be manually activated. To do this, open the **System Preferences** app (or choose **Apple** > **System Preferences**) and then click **Trackpad**. On the following panel you can enable or disable specific gestures and watch instructional videos for each.

Single Click

The entire trackpad on your Mac acts as a mouse button, so you can press down anywhere to "click", activate apps and select items.

Zoom in and out

Place two fingers on the trackpad then pinch them apart to zoom in, or pinch them together to zoom out.

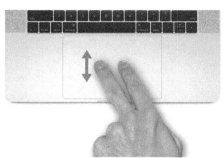

Scroll through pages

If you want to scroll through a document or web page, place two fingers on the trackpad and move them up and down.

Secondary Click

To enable right-click functionality, open the System Preferences app, choose Trackpad, then enable the Secondary click option. Now, whenever you tap on an item with two fingers, you'll activate secondary clicking.

Rotate images

To rotate an image clockwise or anti-clockwise, place two fingers on the trackpad then twist them left or right. This is a tricky gesture so hard to perfect.

Force click

Your trackpad can tell when you tap lightly or tap firmly. That means if you press hard on a link in Safari you can preview the page, or if you press hard on a folder or file you can rename it.

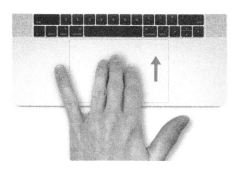

Open Mission Control

To open the macOS Mission Control window place three fingers on the trackpad and move them quickly upwards. You'll then see all your windows slide into a tidy grid.

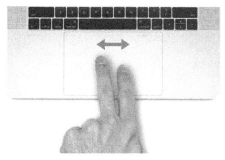

Go back a page in Safari

If you're browsing the web and want to go back a page, swipe from the left to the right with two fingers on the trackpad. Similarly, to go forward a page, swipe right to left.

Access App Expose

Swipe down the trackpad with three fingers and you'll see App Expose appear, letting you jump between windows with a tap.

Go to Launchpad

If you place your thumb and two fingers on the trackpad, then pinch them together, you'll instantly access Launchpad.

Swap between apps

Quickly jump between your open apps by placing three fingers on the trackpad then swiping left or right.

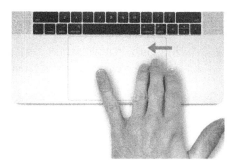

Access Notification Centre

To see your notifications at any time, swipe left from the right edge of the trackpad with two fingers.

Trackpad settings

Scroll, swipe, and click how you like...

The MacBook's trackpad is likely to be one of the best trackpads in the world. It's super sensitive, can support Multi-Touch gestures, and can simulate a "click" using haptic feedback. It's also easy to customise to suit your needs...

An overview of the Trackpad settings panel

To fully customise your Mac's trackpad, open the **System Preferences** app, then click on the **Trackpad** option.

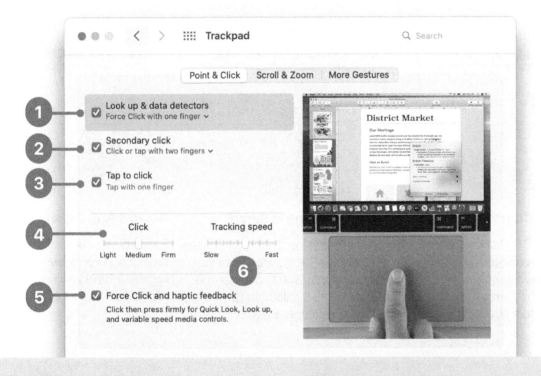

1 Look up & data detectors
With this enabled, you can select a word or a link, then tap on it with three fingers to show information about the word, or see a preview of the link.

2 Secondary link
Turn this on, and you can simulate a "right-click", by tapping on the trackpad with two fingers.

3 Tap to click
Turn this on, and you can click on things by lightly tapping on the trackpad.

4 Click strength
You can use this slider to adjust how hard you need to press on the trackpad to initiate a click.

5 Force Click and haptic feedback
Turn this on, and you can press and hold on something to see more information about it.

6 Tracking speed
This slider determines how quickly the pointer moves around the screen. You can make the trackpad more sensitive by moving the slider to the right, or less sensitive by moving it to the left.

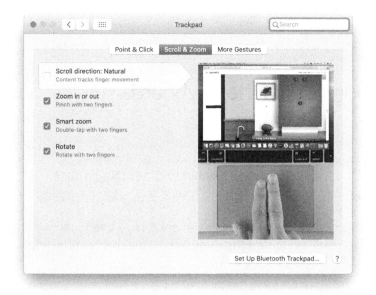

Invert the scroll direction

By default, when you scroll through content (such as a web page) using two fingers, the content will follow the direction of your fingers. This mimics the way touchscreens work, making it a natural way to navigate through content.

If you'd prefer to invert the scrolling direction, so pages scroll downwards when you swipe up, click on the **Scroll & Zoom** tab at the top of the Trackpad settings panel, then untick **Scroll direction: Natural**.

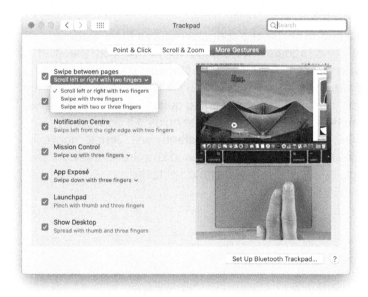

Customise trackpad gestures

While exploring the Trackpad settings panel, click the **More Gestures** tab to discover a number of trackpad gestures (see the previous two pages for an overview of each gesture).

On this panel, you can customise how gestures are initiated. To do this, click the small dropdown arrow to the right of the gesture. You'll then see a handful of options.

Keyboard shortcuts

Discover how to quickly perform actions using the keyboard...

Long before touch screen technology or the mouse came along, the keyboard was king. It was the primary way to interact with any type of computer, whether it was a Mac, a Windows PC, or an IBM machine; so inevitably, a huge number of keyboard shortcuts were devised to save precious time.

Using keyboard shortcuts it's possible to copy and paste, take a screenshot, swap between apps, hide a window and much more. The following two pages will reveal all of these essential shortcuts, plus a few more that will save time and make your Mac even more productive.

The basics

⌘
command

See the button next to the spacebar on your Mac? It should have a looped square symbol in the top corner, then the word *Command* underneath. This is the Command key and it acts as a shortcut for a number of tasks. Take quitting an app for example. If, at any time, you want to quickly quit the current app, press the **Command** key, keep holding it down, then press **Q**. You'll then see the app instantly quit. Simple, right? This method of holding the Command key, then pressing another key, is used for a wide range of tasks.

Common commands

Command-Q: Quit the current app.

Command-A: Select everything on the screen or within a window.

Command-F: Find items within a document. If you're in the Finder you can search your Mac.

Command-O: Open a new file, or a selected file.

Command-S: Save your work or file.

Command-W: Close the current window.

Command-H: Hide the current app or window.

Command-P: Print the current window or page.

Command-Z: Undo whatever action you've just done.

Command-Shift-Z: Redo the Undo action.

Command-Spacebar: Opens Spotlight.

Command-Tab: Switch between open apps.

Option-Command-Esc: Force quit an app.

Command-Shift-3: Take a screenshot.

Command-Shift-4: Capture a specific part of the screen.

Command-Shift-4-Space: Capture the current window or view.

Spacebar: Select a file then press Spacebar to preview it. This includes PDFs, videos, images and more.

Sleep, power and log out

Power button: Press to put your Mac to sleep. Hold down for 1.5 seconds to display a dialog asking if you would like to sleep, restart or shut down. Hold for 5 seconds to force your Mac to shutdown.

Shift-Command-Q: Log out of your user account.

Option-Shift-Command-Q: Log out of your account immediately.

Copy and paste

Copying and pasting is a great way to copy text and content from one app to another. You're basically making a duplicate of the original thing. For example, you could copy your address from the Contacts app, then paste it into Safari; or you could copy a photo from the web and then paste it into an email. The options are endless.

Copy something: Select a file then press **Command-C** to copy it. Alternatively, right-click on it and choose **Copy** in the pop-up window.

Paste something: Next, go to where you want to copy whatever you've selected, then press Command-V to paste it. Alternatively, you can right-click and choose Paste from the pop-up window. You'll see the text, photo, file or folder appear like magic.

Finder commands

Command-D: Duplicate selected file/s.

Command-E: Eject the selected disk or volume.

Command-I: Show the Get Info window for a selected file.

Shift-Command-C: Open the Computer window.

Shift-Command-D: Open the Desktop folder.

Shift-Command-F: Open the All My Files window.

Shift-Command-G: Open a Go to Folder window.

Shift-Command-H: Go to the Home folder of your account.

Shift-Command-I: Open your iCloud Drive.

Shift-Command-K: Open the Network window.

Option-Command-L: Open your Downloads folder.

Shift-Command-O: Open the Documents folder.

Shift-Command-R: Open the AirDrop window.

Control-Shift-Command-T: Add a selected Finder item to the Dock.

Shift-Command-U: Open the Utilities folder.

Control-Command-T: Add the selected item to the sidebar.

Command-J: Show View Options.

Command-K: Open the Connect to Server window.

Command-L: Make an alias of a selected item.

Command-N: Open a new Finder window.

Shift-Command-N: Create a new folder.

Option-Command-N: Create a new Smart Folder.

Command-R: Show the original file for an alias.

Command-Y: Use Quick Look to preview a file.

Command-1: View items in a Finder window as icons.

Command-2: View items in a Finder window as a list.

Command-3: View items in a Finder window as columns.

Command-4: View items in a Finder window with Cover Flow.

Command–Mission Control: Show the desktop.

Option–double-click: Open a folder in a separate window.

Command–double-click: Open a folder in a separate tab or window.

Command-Delete: Move selected item to the Trash.

Shift-Command-Delete: Empty the Trash.

Special characters, accents and symbols

Learn how to find emojis, symbols, and more...

Every now and then you might need to enter a special character in a document, or within an app. It might be an accent used by a foreign language, such as an acute symbol, a diaeresis, or an underbar.

Finding these characters on your keyboard can be tricky, because they're not always labeled, but thankfully, it's really easy to explore and apply these accents: just hold down the corresponding letter, then choose the correct accent via the pop-up field. Here's what it looks like when you hold down the e character when typing an email:

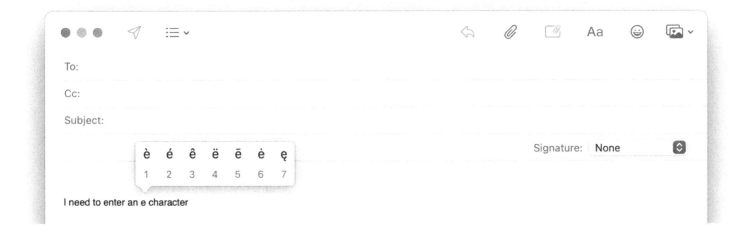

Shortcuts

For special characters and symbols, however, you'll need to search the web, find a manual, or be lucky enough to guess the right combination. To save you the trouble, here are the shortcuts you need to type a variety of special characters and symbols on your Mac:

?: Shift-/	**%**: Shift-5	**©**: Option-G
!: Shift-1	**&**: Shift-7	**®**: Option-R
@: Shift-2	*****: Shift-8	**™**: Shift-Option-2
£: Shift-3	**#**: Option-3	: Shift-Option-K
$: Shift-4	**∞**: Option-5	**π**: Option-P
€: Option-3	**•**: Option-8	**ø**: Option-O

Use the Character Viewer to explore and insert symbols, pictographs, emoji, and punctuation

If you'd like to explore all the characters, accents, symbols and pictographs available on your Mac, or if you're looking for something very specific, then the Character Viewer is a great tool for searching and inserting characters.

To display the Character Viewer, click the place within a document or message where you want the character to appear, then press **Control–Command–Spacebar**. The Character Viewer will then appear. Click the icon in the top-right corner to expand it like this:

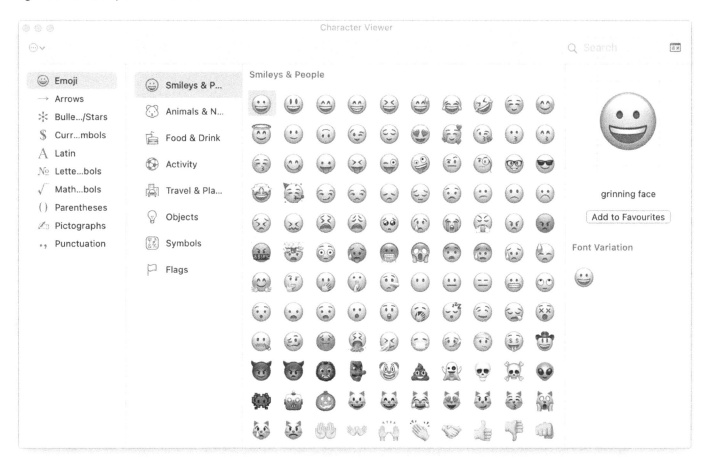

When you find the character you need, just click on it to insert it into your document or message.

Change the desktop wallpaper

Give the Desktop background a fresh coat of paint...

One of the easiest ways to customise your Mac is to change the desktop wallpaper image. There are dozens to choose from, and you can even use a photo of your own. To get started:

1 **Right-click** on the current desktop wallpaper, then choose **Change Desktop Background**.

2 Alternatively, open the **System Preferences** app, then click on **Desktop & Screen Saver**.

The Desktop & Screen Saver panel will then appear:

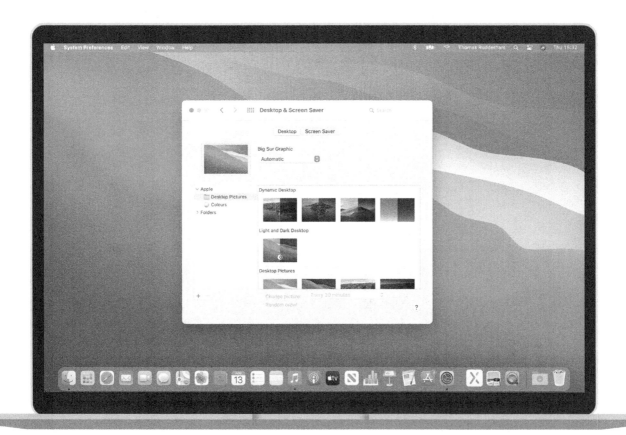

Select a new wallpaper

Click on **Desktop Pictures** to choose an image supplied by Apple.

Choose **Colours** if you'd like to apply a sold colour background to your desktop.

Alternatively, click on any of the options under **Photos** or **Folders** to choose a personal image saved on your Mac.

Use a Dynamic wallpaper

A dynamic wallpaper will change its appearance to suit the time of day. So when you turn on your Mac in the morning you'll see sunlit dunes, while at night you'll see them lit by the stars. To enable this subtle but evocative wallpaper:

1 Open the **System Preferences** app, then click on **Desktop & Screen Saver**.

2 Click on **Desktop Pictures**, then look for the images labelled as **Dynamic Desktop**.

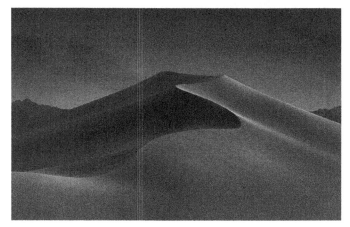

Use a screen saver

Lock and hide the desktop, but leave the screen on while you're away...

A screen saver is an animated sequence that plays out across the display whenever you're not using it. There are a few advantages to running a screensaver while you're not using the Mac:

- It's a helpful way to remind yourself that the Mac is still running.
- It prevents anyone else from seeing what's on the screen when you're not there.
- It can prevent "burn-in" from happening. This is where a stationery item (such as the dock or menu), becomes burned into the screen when it has been displayed for a long period of time. Don't worry however, as this only happens on older external displays.

Set up a screen saver:

1 Right-click on the current desktop wallpaper, choose **Change Desktop Background**, then when the **Desktop & Screen Saver** panel appears, click the **Screen Saver** tab near the top of the window.

2 Alternatively, open the **System Preferences** app, click on **Desktop & Screen Saver,** then click **Screen Saver.**

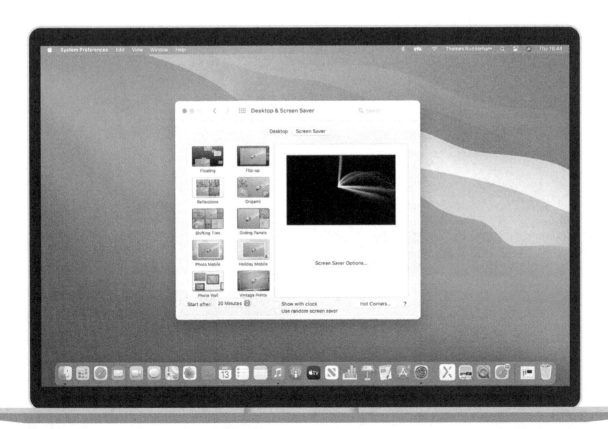

Select a screen saver

Look in the left-hand panel, and you'll see several screen savers to choose from.

Click on a screen saver, and you'll see an animated preview of it on the right.

You have now selected a new screen saver.

Customise a screen saver

  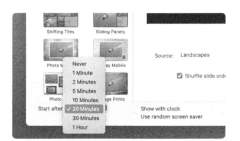

Select a screen saver in the left-hand panel.

You can use the drop-down menu below the preview to select a source of images, or to customise the screen saver.

You can also specify how long it takes for the screen saver to activate by using the **Start after** drop-down in the bottom-left corner.

Activate the screen saver using a "Hot Corner"

By assigning a corner of the screen as a "Hot Corner", you can activate the screen saver at any time by moving the cursor into that corner. Here's how it works:

1 Select a screen saver, then click the **Hot Corner...** button in the bottom-right corner of the panel.

2 In the pop-up window, select a corner of the screen, then use the drop-down menu to select **Start Screen Saver**. Click **OK** to save your preference.

3 To activate the screen saver, move the cursor into the corner you've chosen, and it will immediately begin.

4 Move the cursor or press a key to stop the screen saver. You may need to re-enter your password to return to the desktop.

Swap between Dark and Light Mode

Enable Dark Mode, change colours and more...

macOS has a beautiful, simple interface, but if you *really* look at it, you'll notice that it's mostly made up of white panels and windows. If you'd like to give your Mac a fresh coat of paint, then it's possible to enable Dark Mode, which gives all of those panels and windows an evocative dark appearance. Here's a comparison of the System Preferences app to give you with an idea:

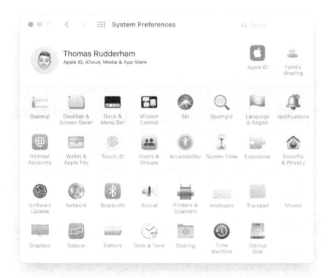 

How to toggle Dark Mode on or off

All of Apple's built-in apps get the Dark Mode treatment, including Safari, Mail, Photos, Contacts, Calendar, Reminders, Notes and more. To enable Dark Mode:

1. Open the System Preferences app. You'll find it in the Dock, but you can also find it by clicking the **Apple** logo at the top of the screen then **System Preferences**...

2. Click on **General**, then click on **Dark** in the Appearances section.

3. If you'd like Dark Mode to activate at nighttime, rather than all the time, then choose the **Auto** option.

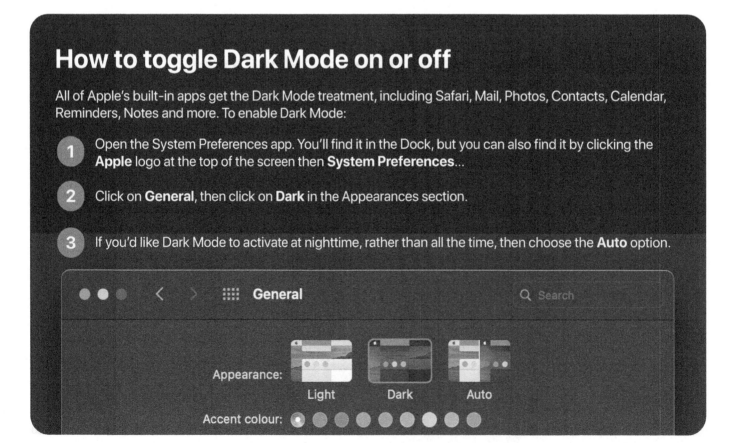

How Dark Mode works in some of the built-in apps

Some apps on your Mac have special Dark Mode settings:

- **Mail:** If you'd rather use a light background for emails, open the **Mail** app, click on **Mail** in the Apple Menu, then choose **Preferences**. Click the **Viewing** tab, then deselect **Use dark backgrounds for messages**.

- **Maps.** To use a light background for the Maps view, click on **View** in the Apple Menu, then click **Use Dark Map**.

- **Notes**. To use a light background for your notes, click on **Notes** in the Apple Menu, click on **Preferences**, then deselect **Use dark backgrounds for note content**.

- **TextEdit**. If you'd like to use a light background for documents, open **TextEdit**, click on **View** in the Apple Menu, then click **Use Dark Background for Windows**.

Change the accent colour

Whenever you click on a menu option or select text, macOS will highlight it with a blue colour. If you'd rather see a different shade:

1. Open the **System Preferences** app, then click **General.**

2. Look for **Accent Colour**, it's near the top of the panel.

3. Click on a coloured circle to select a new accent colour. There are eight to choose from: blue, purple, pink, red, orange, yellow, green, or grey.

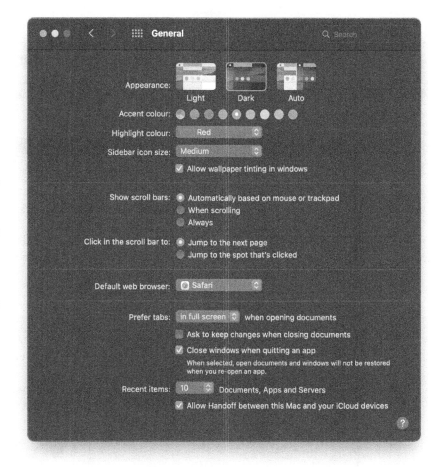

Use Mission Control

Arrange your working space across multiple desktops...

If you use your Mac for multiple distinct purposes (such as work and home), then it's a good idea to start using Mission Control. It works by enabling you to create multiple desktops, called *spaces*, to organise your apps and windows.

How to activate Mission Control

There are many ways you can activate Mission Control:

- Press the **F3** button on the MacBook Air keyboard. Notice it has the Mission Control icon above it:
- Press the **function** key, then **F3**.
- Swipe up with three fingers across the trackpad.
- Click on the **Launchpad** icon in the Dock, then open **Mission Control**.

After activating Mission Control, you'll see all the apps and windows open on your Mac:

Jump between spaces

To jump from one desktop space to another, open **Mission Control** then click on the space at the top of the screen:

Add a new desktop space

To add a new desktop space to Mission Control, click the **plus** button (**+**) in the top-right corner:

A new desktop space will then appear. You can open apps and folders within this space, and they will remain here, making it easy to start organising your apps and folders into multiple spaces.

Assign an app to a specific space

If you'd like an app to open in a specific space - rather than all of them - use Mission Control to visit the space you'd like to assign the app, right-click on its icon in the Dock, then choose **Options** > **This Desktop**.

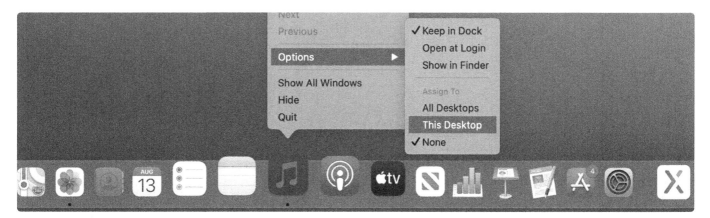

Delete a desktop space

To delete a space, activate Mission Control, move the cursor over the space you wish to delete, then click the **close** (**x**) button:

Make the screen bigger or smaller

Change the size of everything on the screen to suit your vision and needs...

When you first set up your MacBook, the desktop, folders, apps, text and icons are all sized at a comfortable level for someone with normal vision. The trouble is, not everyone has perfect eyesight, so those average-sized icons and sentences might be hard to see. Thankfully, there's a straightforward System Preferences panel for adjusting the size of *everything* on your Mac's screen. Here's how it works:

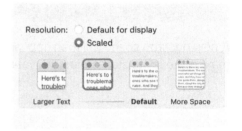

1 Start by opening the **System Preferences** app, then click on **Displays**.

2 On the Display tab, look for a small boxed area called **Scaled**.

3 Try clicking on the different boxes to zoom the entire screen in and out. After some experimentation you should find a zoom level that's comfortable for you. Look across the page to see how the different sizes affect the view...

Make icons bigger or smaller

Every file and folder on your Mac is displayed using an icon that's 64 by 64 pixels in size. Basically, they're postage stamp sized. To make them bigger or smaller:

1 Go to the Finder or Desktop on your Mac, then click **View** in the menu at the top of the screen, then choose **Show View Options**.

2 In the pop-up window, drag the **Icon Size** slider to the right to increase icon and folder sizes, or to the left to shrink them.

Larger Text

Large Text

Default

More Space

What is iCloud

Learn what iCloud is all about...

iCloud enables you to sync all of your photos, documents, music, apps, contacts, calendars and much more across your Apple devices.

This means you can snap a photo on your iPhone then see it automatically appear on your Mac, PC or Television. It means you can purchase a song, movie or TV show in iTunes and see it appear on all of your devices. It also means you can start writing a document on your Mac, edit it on your iPhone and see the changes appear simultaneously across both devices. Here's a quick overview of some of the other features found within iCloud:

Photos

Any photo taken on your iPad or iPhone is wirelessly uploaded to iCloud, then automatically downloaded onto your other devices, Mac, or PC. So if you take a photo during the day on your iPhone, when you get home you'll see it waiting for you on our Mac, all without having to sync devices or use wires.

iCloud Drive

iCloud Drive automatically saves all your documents and desktop files. This means you can access them from another device, or a web browser via www.icloud.com. iCloud Drive also works with Pages, Numbers, and Keynote, so if you're writing a letter or creating a presentation on your Mac, you'll be able to continue editing it on your iPad or iPhone without having to worry about transferring the file. Edits are automatically updated across all of your devices.

Find My iPhone (for Mac)

If you can't find your iPhone, iPad, or Mac, the Find My iPhone feature in iCloud will enable you to locate it. By signing into your iCloud account, either from www.icloud.com or another iPhone, you can see all your devices on a map, set a passcode lock, remotely wipe them or send a message to the screen. You can also enable Lost Mode, whereby the device is automatically locked, a message with a contact appears on the screen, and the device automatically reports its location via iCloud.

Safari

iCloud automatically saves your bookmarks, Reading Lists and open tabs. So if you begin reading a lengthy web article on your Mac, you can continue reading it at a later time on your iPad or iPhone.

Mac Backups

iCloud automatically backs up your Mac when it's plugged into a power source and connected to the web over Wi-Fi. iCloud backs up the following things: your desktop, folders and files, music, movies and TV shows, photos and videos, settings, app data and messages. If you buy a new Mac, then you can restore all of the above by using an existing iCloud backup.

Find My iPhone (for Mac)

Find your Mac using another computer or iOS device...

If the worst happens, and you lose your MacBook, first of all, don't panic! It might be somewhere obvious, like in another room, in a cupboard, or sitting on the table of a coffee shop (okay, that is a little worrying). If you've looked around and still can't find it, then here's how to track it down using iCloud, and even remotely erase its hard drive...

Use Find My iPhone to find your MacBook Air

The easiest way to find your Mac is to use Find My iPhone, a feature of iCloud which tracks all of your devices and displays them on a map. Here's how it works:

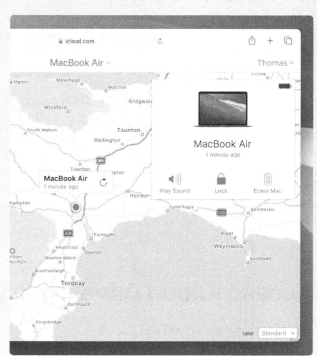

1 Use another device or computer and go to www.icloud.com.

2 Try to log in. If two-factor authentication is enabled and you're asked for a passcode, use your iPhone or iPad to get the code and enter it.

3 Once you're logged into iCloud, click the Find iPhone icon, then wait for your devices to load.

4 Click on your MacBook using the Map screen, or click the drop-down icon at the top of the screen and select it. In the pop-up panel you'll be able to play a sound, lock your Mac or erase it. See below for more details.

Erase your Mac

If the worst has happened and you don't think you'll be able to get your Mac back, then you can securely erase its contents to prevent someone from accessing your data. When erased an activation lock is enabled and Find My iPhone is automatically turned on. This means if if your Mac is ever restored by someone else you can still track it and be assured that they can't unlock it without your Apple ID and password.
After you've selected Erase:

- If it's online then your Mac will be immediately erased, and you'll get a confirmation email to let you know.
- If it's offline then it will be erased when it's next turned on. If you manage to find your Mac before it's turned on then you can cancel the erase by logging into iCloud, selecting your Mac then choosing Stop Erase Request.
- If it's erased and then you find it, you can restore the most recent backup from TimeMachine during the set-up process.

iCloud Drive

Store all your files, settings and media in the cloud...

Using iCloud Drive, you can store all your documents and desktop files in iCloud, then access them at any time using another device, such as your iPad, iPhone, or even a Windows computer using www.icloud.com. Not only does this make working across multiple devices easier, but it also means you have a backup of your entire Mac available, at any time.

Set up iCloud Drive

This part is easy. Just open the **System Preferences** app, select **iCloud**, then click **iCloud Drive**. The first time you enable iCloud Drive, you'll be asked to upgrade your iCloud account to support this feature. All this does is move any of your files from iCloud to iCloud Drive.

Once iCloud has been enabled, click the **Options**... button to the right of iCloud Drive, then click **Desktop & Documents Folders**.

Because you're storing your documents in iCloud, whenever you save a file or make a change, that file will be uploaded to iCloud using your network connection. Keep this in mind, because if you save a very large file to your Mac, it will be automatically uploaded to iCloud in the background and could, potentially, slow down your web connection.

Access iCloud Drive using your Mac

Whenever you want to access iCloud Drive using the Finder, open a new window then click the **iCloud Drive** shortcut in the sidebar.

You'll see folders for accessing your documents and desktop via iCloud, plus a selection of folders containing any files you have created using Pages, Numbers, or Keynote.

Anything you to add to these folders is automatically synced via iCloud to all your devices. Similarly, if you delete anything, it is also deleted across all of your devices.

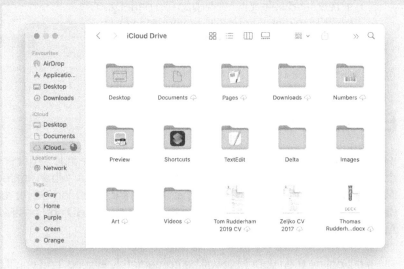

Access iCloud Drive on the web

Because iCloud works across the web, you can access your iCloud Drive from anywhere in the world using a desktop web browser. Just head over to **www.icloud. com**, sign in using your Apple ID, and click the **iCloud Drive** button.

To download a file, select it then click the **Download** button at the top of the screen (it looks like a cloud with an arrow pointing down). To download multiple files, hold down the **Command** key on your keyboard, select the files, then click the **Download** button.

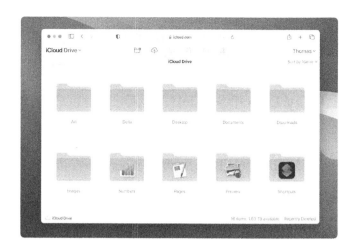

Access iCloud Drive using your iPhone or iPad

If you own an iPhone or iPad, then you can also access iCloud Drive to view and save files from your Documents and Desktop folder. To do this open the **Files** app on your iPhone or iPad, tap on any files you wish to open, then tap the **Share** button to save them locally to the device.

What happens when you turn iCloud Drive off

If you turn iCloud Drive off, anything saved on your Desktop and Documents folder is automatically cleared. Nothing is actually deleted, however. Instead, those files remain within your iCloud Drive.

There are two ways you can restore your files from iCloud Drive back to their original location, both are a bit of a hassle:

Use iCloud Drive via the Finder

1. Open a Finder window, then click **iCloud Drive** in the sidebar.

2. Open the iCloud Documents folder, then select everything by pressing **Command-A** on your keyboard. Next, press **Command-C** to copy them.

3. Open the **Documents** folder on your Mac, then press **Command-V** to paste the files.

4. Depending on the number of files and your network connection speed, the files should download from iCloud Drive to your Mac in a short period of time.

Use iCloud.com

If you would rather use a browser to locate your files, then:

1. Visit **www.icloud.com** using your web browser.

2. Select **iCloud Drive**.

3. Double-click on the **Documents** folder.

4. Select a file, then click the **Download** button near the top of the window to save it to your Mac.

5. To select multiple files, hold down the **Command** key and click on them.

Safari tabs, bookmarks and history

Enjoy a consistent experience across the web from device to device...

With iCloud enabled on your Mac, iPhone, and iPad, you can share the same browser history, bookmarks, and tabs across Safari on all of your devices. This means you can start reading a page on your Mac, then later pick it up on your iPhone.

Set up iCloud for Safari

Before you begin, make sure you're signed into iCloud on all of your devices. To do this on your Mac, open **System Preferences**, select **iCloud**, enter your Apple ID and password, then click **Sign In**. iCloud for Safari should be automatically enabled. If it isn't:

1 Open **System Preferences**.

2 Click on **Apple ID**.

3 Click on **Safari** to enable it.

How to use iCloud Tabs

1 When you're using your Mac to browse the web, you can see any open tabs on your other devices by clicking the Tabs button in the top-right corner:

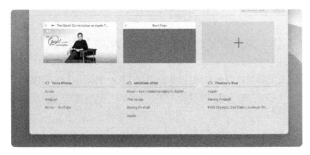

2 The window will change to show all your open tabs. Along the bottom will be a list of the tabs open on your other devices:

iCloud Bookmarks

Bookmarks are helpful shortcuts to all of your favorite websites. Using iCloud, these bookmarks will appear across all of your Apple devices, so you only need to add a bookmark once and it will appear within Safari on your Mac, iPhone, and iPad.

To see your iCloud bookmarks, open **Safari**, click **View** in the menu at the top of the screen, then choose **Show Bookmarks Sidebar**. A sidebar will then slide into view to display any bookmarks you have saved.

To add a new bookmark, visit the website you wish to add, then press **Command-D** on your keyboard. You can also click on **Bookmarks** in the top menu and choose **Add Bookmark**. A small menu will slide down the screen enabling you to enter a bookmark name and description.

To remove a bookmark, open the bookmark sidebar, find the bookmark you wish to remove, right-click on it, then choose **Delete**.

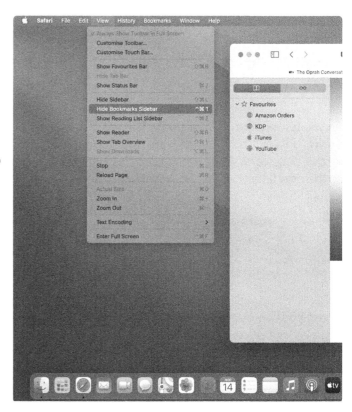

iCloud Browsing History

Whenever you visit a website in Safari, a log of that visit is stored in your browser's history, which you can access by pressing Command-Y on your keyboard.

With iCloud, your browsing history is stored across all of your Apple devices, so if you visit a website on your iPhone, then later open Safari on your Mac, you can see a log of that visit.

iCloud History is a helpful feature that makes browsing the web more seamless across all of your Apple devices, but if you would like to disable it:

1 Open **System Preferences**.

2 Click on **Apple ID**.

3 Untick **Safari** to disable iCloud History, Tabs, and Bookmarks.

Manage passwords saved in Safari

Reference, update, and delete your saved passwords...

As you browse the internet, you're likely to start registering for accounts across websites and cloud-based services. As you do, you'll be asked to enter personal details (such as your email address and telephone number), along with a unique password. Whenever you do this, Safari will automatically save your username, email address, and password, so the next time you visit the website you can login by using your fingerprint or Mac's password, in a small box which looks like this:

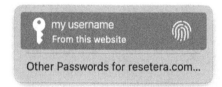

These passwords are saved within Safari, and also automatically synced with any iPads, iPhones, and other Macs that you may own. If you later return to a website or service and update your password, it will automatically be saved and synced across all of your devices.

How to access your saved passwords

To access all of the passwords saved within Safari:

1 Click on **Safari** in the Apple menu, then choose **Preferences**.

2 Click on the **Passwords** tab. After entering your user account password, you'll see all the usernames and passwords saved within Safari:

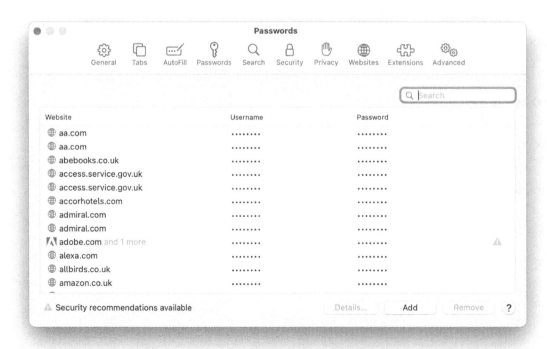

View or edit a password

Double-click on a username or password within the window and a small panel will appear. In this panel you can view and edit both the username and password.

Delete a password

Select a username and password from the list then click **Remove** at the bottom of the window.

Duplicate passwords

It's never a good idea to use the same password across multiple websites, especially if you use the same email address or username. While browsing the Passwords panel, you'll be warned of any duplicate passwords by a yellow triangle. If you see one, it's a good idea to visit the website associated with the password and then change it immediately. To look for duplicate passwords:

1. Click on **Safari** in the Apple menu, then choose **Preferences**.

2. Click on the **Passwords** tab. After entering your user account password, you'll see all the usernames and passwords saved within Safari.

3. Look for any yellow triangles next to passwords.

4. Click on a triangle, and you'll see a blue link, this will take you to the relevant website associated with the username and password. From there you'll be able to update the password and ensure it's unique to that website.

Tip! Let Safari generate unique passwords

When a websites asks you to enter a new password, click on the Password text field, then use Safari's AutoFill password generator create a password for you. Safari will generate a password that's nearly impossible to guess, save it for you, then automatically enter the password when you return to the same website.

Use Safari to browse the web

Visit websites, organise tabs, customise your experience, and more...

Safari is the very best way to browse the web on your Mac. It's blazingly fast, rendering web pages in an instant. It supports Apple Pay, so you can make purchases on the web without entering your credit card details, it can strip all the ads and junk out of a page to show you only the content you want to see, it can automatically block pop-ups and so much more.

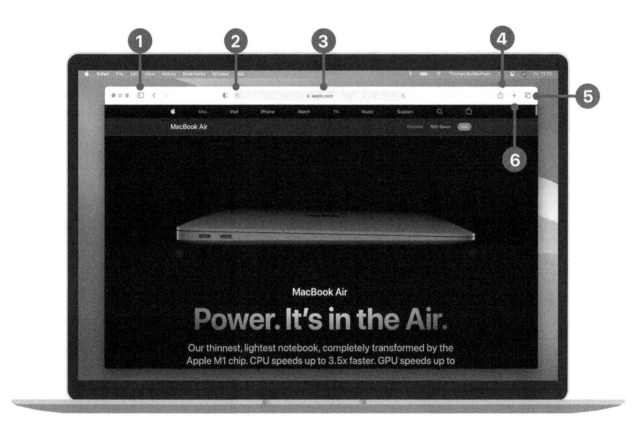

The basics

1 Click the **Sidebar** button to show your favorite websites and saved bookmarks.

2 Click the **Reader** button to view an article without adverts and clutter.

3 Click on the **address bar** to enter a website's address, or to search Google (see across page for more details).

4 Click the **Share** button to send a webpage to another Mac, message a link, email a link, or print the page.

5 Click the **New Tab** button to open a new tabbed view.

6 Click the **Tabs** button to view all of the tabs open on your Mac.

Visit a website

Open Safari for the first time and you'll see a blank canvas. To visit a website, just click on the **address bar** at the top of the screen, then enter its web address; for example, www.apple.com.

Search the web

The address bar in Safari also acts as a search engine, so to search the web for any question or search term, just type your query into the address bar at the top of the screen.

Search suggestions

As you type into the address bar, notice that Safari offers search suggestions in real-time. Click on a suggestion to confirm your query.

Tabs

Tabs make it possible to have multiple websites or web pages open in the same window. This is useful for when you need to keep a page open for reference while reading another, or for quickly jumping between regularly used websites.

- **To open a new tab:** Press **Command-T** on your keyboard, or click the small **plus** button in the very top-right corner of Safari.

- **To close a tab:** Press **Command-W** on the keyboard, or hover the cursor over the tab then click the small **x** button in its top left corner.

- **To see an overview of all your tabs:** Click the **Show all tabs** button in the very top-right corner of the screen. You'll see all your tabs zoom out and arrange themselves in a grid layout. To jump to another tab, simply click on it.

Show tab icons

Sometimes, when you have dozens of tabs open, it can be hard to go back to a specific website. You can either read the page titles in each tab, or go through them one at a time until the right tab appears. To make this easier, you can enable tab icons within Safari. Once activated, each tab will include a small logo of the website to the left of the tab text. To enable tab icons:

1. Click **Safari** in the menu at the top of the screen.

2. Choose **Preferences**.

3. Click the **Tabs** button.

4. Select **Show website icons in tabs**.

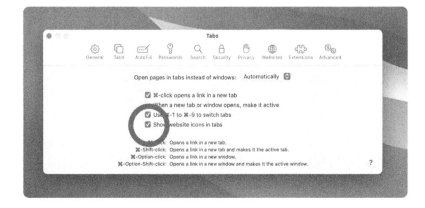

Use multiple windows

If you'd like to view two websites at once, then press **Command-N** on your keyboard, or go to **File > New Window** in the Finder menu.

Turn a tab into a new window

If you would like to turn one of your tabs into its own window, simply click on the tab then drag it away from the others. When you let go it will turn into a new window.

Merge multiple windows

To merge multiple windows into one, click on **Window** in the Finder menu and choose **Merge All Windows**. All your open windows will now turn into tabs within a single window.

Customise the Safari Start Page

Whenever you open a new tab or window, Safari will display the Start Page. From here, you can see the following items:

- Your bookmarked webpages.
- Frequently visited websites that aren't bookmarked.
- Suggested websites based on your browsing history.
- A brief privacy report, detailing how many trackers have been blocked over the last seven days.
- Any tabs open on your other Apple devices.

To customise the look of the start page, click the **settings** button in the bottom-right corner. A small pop-up window will then appear, enabling you to toggle items on or off, and even add a background image to the Start Page.

Use Safari Reader to remove clutter on web pages

Often, when you visit a website, it can be hard to focus on the content of a page because of distracting adverts, images, and layout. Safari has a great feature called Safari Reader, which removes all the clutter from a web page to leave you with just the content you came to see. To enable Safari Reader, load a web page, then click the **Safari Reader** button within the address bar.

Customise Safari Reader

While using Safari Reader, it's possible to tweak the font, background colour and text size. To do this just click the **aA** icon in the address bar.

Use Safari Reader all the time

If you'd like to use Safari Reader every time you visit a specific web page, hold down the **Control** key and click the **Safari Reader** button in the address bar. When the pop-up window appears choose **Use Reader Automatically on [website]**.

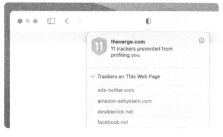

See a privacy report

You can quickly see how many trackers were blocked on a website by clicking the **shield** icon next to the address bar. To see more information, click the **info** button in the upper-right corner.

Search a web page for text

Looking for a keyword, name or figure on a web page? By pressing **Command-F** you can search a web page for anything text-based.

Enable Private Browsing

You can browse the web without saving any history, searches, passwords or field entries by enabling Private Browsing mode. To do this, go to **File** > **New Private Window**, or press **Shift-Command-N**.

Change the search engine

If you'd rather search the web using Yahoo!, Bing, or DuckDuckGo, go to **Safari** > **Preferences** > **Search**, then choose a new provider using the **Search engine** drop-down menu.

Clear your browsing history

If you need to clear your browsing history, click on **History** > **Show All History,** then click the **Clear History** button in the upper-right corner. In the pop-up window, choose the duration of time you'd like to clear, then click **Clear History**.

Check your email

Compose messages, organise your inbox, and more...

Having your own email address is pretty much a requirement for using the web today. You need an email address to register website accounts, make purchases and receive messages and notifications... basically any productive task involved with using the web. Thankfully, the Mail app in macOS is brilliant. It's designed with a clean interface that helps you focus on what's important: your emails.

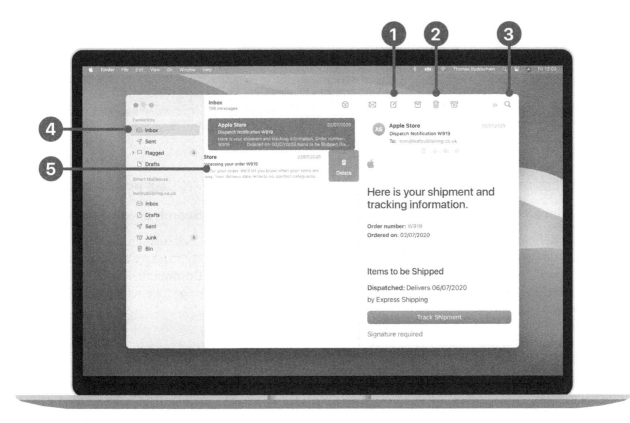

The basics

1 Create a new email by clicking this button in the upper-left corner of the screen.

2 These shortcut buttons enable you to delete an email, reply, forward, flag, archive, or move an email to another folder.

3 Click on the **Search** button to (you guessed it) search through your emails. You can look for people, email content, dates, or attachments.

4 You can navigate through multiple accounts and folders using the sidebar.

5 Move the cursor over an email, then swipe horizontally with two fingers across the trackpad or Magic Mouse. Swipe towards the left and you'll be able to delete the email in an instant. Swipe towards the right and you'll be able to mark it as Unread.

Set up Mail

Open the Mail app for the first time and you'll be prompted to add an account. To get started, choose your email provider from the list provided, then click **Continue**.

Enter your details

On the following screen, enter your name, email address, and email password, then click **Create** to set up your account.

Sync mail, contacts and more

Once your account has been added, you'll automatically see your inbox appear. To customise the account or remove it, open the **System Preferences** app then click on **Internet Accounts**.

Send an email to multiple recipients

To create a new email, press **Command-N**, click the **New Message** button in the Mail toolbar, or choose **File** > **New Message**.

When you type someone's name or email into the **To:** field, the Mail app will automatically help to complete their address by looking through your Contacts and message history. Once you've entered an address, you can add another by using a comma to separate addresses.

Format text in an email

To format text within an email, click the **Format** button at the top of the message window (**Aa**), then use the controls to format your text. It's possible to change the font, size, colour, alignment, style, indentation and background colour.

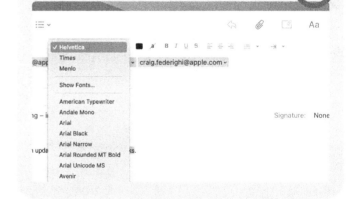

Attach an image

There are a couple of ways to attach an image with an email:

1. Click the **photo** button in the top-right corner, then either choose a photo from your library, or take on using your iPhone or iPad.

2. Drag a photo from the desktop or a folder onto the email window.

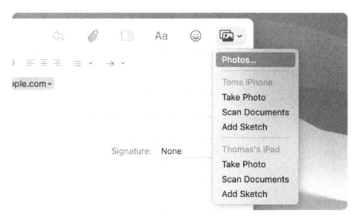

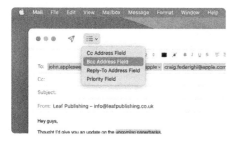

View Cc and Bcc fields

If you'd like to show the carbon copy (cc) and blind carbon copy (bcc) fields, simply click the **list view** button in the top-left corner of the draft window.

Embed a web link into text

To embed a web link into a piece of text, highlight the text, **right-click**, then choose **Link > Add Link**. In the pop-up field, enter the link URL, then click **OK**.

Manage or add a signature

Closing off an email with a signature is a professional way of letting people know how they can reach you. To manage your signatures, or add a new one, click on the **Signature** drop-down in the upper-right corner of the draft email, then choose **Edit Signatures**.

Include an emoji

Sending an emoji to someone is a fun way to add humour to an email. To explore and add an emoji:

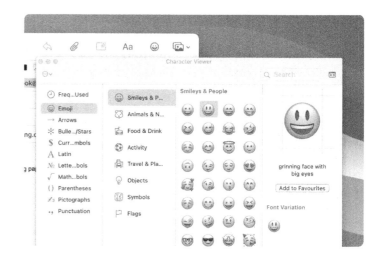

1 Click the **Emoji** button in the top-right corner of the email draft window.

2 Explore the emojis by scrolling through the pop-up window, or use the search field to find an exact match.

3 Double click on the emoji you want to use, and it will be inserted into the email.

Add an attachment

To add an attachment, click the **Attach** button at the top of the message window (it looks like a paperclip), then choose the file on your Mac.

Delete multiple emails at once

To delete more than one email at once, hold down the **Command** key, then click on the emails you wish to remove. Once you've selected them all, press the **delete** button on your keyboard.

Mark a message as spam

If you've received an email that you didn't expect or sign-up for, then select it and hit the **Spam** button at the top of the Mail window. Any similar messages from the same recipient will automatically be moved to the Spam mailbox.

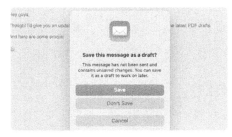

Save a draft email

While composing an email, click the **close** button and Mail will ask if you would like to save the message as a draft. You can find all your draft emails in the sidebar on the left.

Save a contact

To save a contact's email address to your Mac, hover the cursor over their name at the top of the email, click the small arrow which appears then choose **Add to Contacts**.

Annotate a photo or PDF

While composing an email with an image or PDF attachment, you can use Markup to add sketches, shapes, a signature and text. To do this hover the cursor over the attachment, click the small **arrow** in the top-right corner then choose **Markup**.

Create a Smart Mailbox

You can tell the Mail app to automatically sort incoming messages into unique folders. For example, you can tell it to sort all the messages from family members into a "Family" mailbox, or you can ask it to send all your bank statements into a mailbox called "Statements". Here's how it works:

1 Search for a word or term using the Search box in the top-right corner.

2 Click the **plus (+)** button at the top of the search results panel.

3 In the panel which appears, give your Smart Mailbox a name.

4 Use the various options to tell Mail how to filter incoming messages into the new mailbox.

Chat using Messages

Send messages, photos, videos, emojis and more...

So you might have noticed the Messages app on your Mac, and you're wondering what it's for? Well, it's the same Messages app as the one on your iPhone, which means you can sent text messages from your Mac to a friend or family member. It's also possible to send videos, drawings and animated messages.

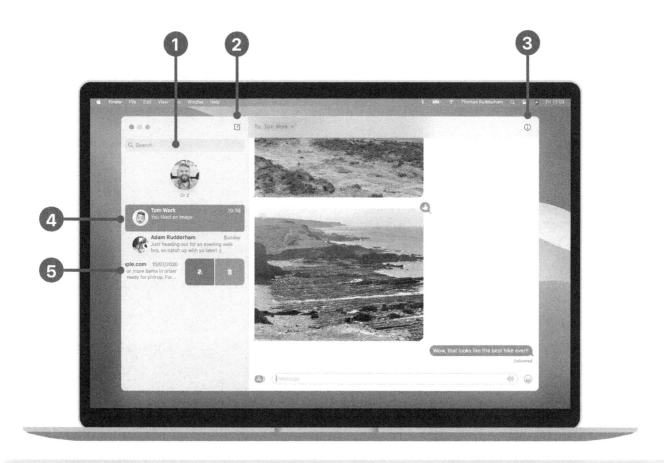

The basics

1 Use the search bar to look for people, keywords, or attachments.

2 To begin a new conversation with someone, just click the **New** button in the upper-left corner.

3 Click on the **info (i)** button to start a phone or video call, mute someone or see any shared attachments.

4 You can right-click on a conversation to delete it, mute the person, or open the chat in a separate window.

5 Swipe across a conversation (using either the trackpad or Magic Mouse) to mute alerts or delete it.

How to send a message

To send your very first message:

1 Click the **new message** button in the top-right corner of the sidebar.

2 In the **To**: field, start typing the name of someone in your Contacts book, or the phone number of someone you know.

3 Enter your message in the iMessage field at the bottom of the window, then press the **Enter** key to send the message.

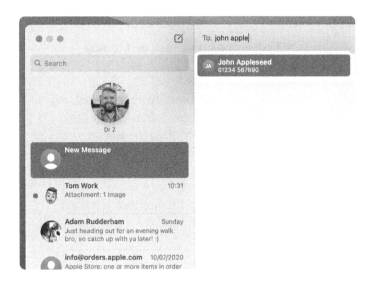

Delete a conversation

There are a few ways to remove a chat conversation:
- **Swipe right-to-left** across the chat conversation in the sidebar.
- **Right-click** on the conversation in the sidebar, then click **Delete Conversation...**
- Select the conversation in the sidebar, click **File** in the menu at the top of the screen, then choose **Delete Conversation...**

Pin conversations

If you chat to someone on a regular basis, then it's a good idea to pin their conversation to the top of the sidebar. That way you can quickly find them without having to search or scroll through the sidebar. To pin someone:
- **Swipe left-to-right** across the chat conversation in the sidebar, then click the yellow pin button.
- **Right-click** on the conversation in the sidebar, then click **Pin.**

Send a Memoji Sticker

Think of Memoji Stickers as custom-made Emojis, but with more expressions

1 Click the **App (A)** button to the left of the iMessage field at the bottom of the screen.

2 In the pop-up window, click on **Memoji Stickers**.

3 A larger pop-up window will appear, enabling you to choose from several pre-made Memoji's. Scroll horizontally to select a Memoji face, or scroll vertically to choose an expression.

4 When you've found a Memoji that you like, **double-clic**k on it to send it.

Create your very own Memoji Sticker

Using the Messages app, it's possible to create your very own Memoji. You can select from hundreds of options, including hairstyles, head shapes, eyewear, and headgear, to create a Memoji that looks just like yourself; or something totally unique. Here's how it works:

1 Click the **App (A)** button to the left of the iMessage field at the bottom of the screen.

2 In the pop-up window, click on **Memoji Stickers**, then click the **plus (+)** button in the top-left corner of the pop-up window.

3 Use the Memoji creator tool to create your very own Memoji. Use the sidebar to navigate the various options, then scroll vertically through the panel on the right to make a choice.

4 Click the blue **Done** button when you've finished creating your custom-made Memoji. It will appear in the Memoji Sticker window, with various expressions for you to choose from.

Send an emoji

To send a regular emoji, click on the grey **Emoji** button next in the bottom-right corner. A pop-up window will appear, letting you scroll vertically through a massive number of emojis.

If there's a specific emoji that you're looking for, try using the search field at the top of the pop-up window to find it.

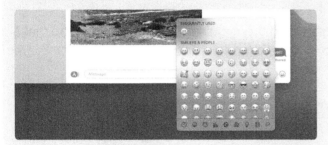

Send an audio message

Sending an audio message to someone is both quicker than typing, while also being more personal. To do this, click on the **audio** button in the bottom-right corner, then start talking out loud. When you've finished saying your message, click the red **stop** button; then to send the audio message, click the blue **arrow** button.

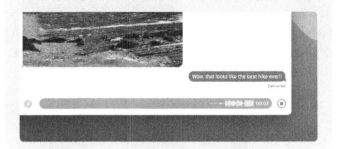

Add a Tapback sticker

To add a personal touch to a delivered message, **right-click** on the message and choose **Tapback...** You can then choose from six stickers, which will be seen by both parties.

See more about a conversation

While viewing a conversation, click the **Info (i)** button in the top-right corner. In the pop-up window you'll be able to call or email the person, share your location, hide any more alerts, and see media attachments.

Adjust text size

If you're struggling to read the text within a conversation, click on **View** in the menu, then select **Make Text Bigger**. You can keep adjusting text until it's large enough, or revert it back to its default size

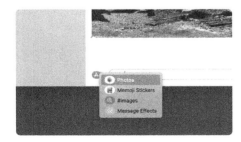

Send a photo or video

To send a photo with a message, click the **App (A)** button and choose **Photos**. In the pop-up window, select a photo from your library, then double-click to send it.

Send a full-screen effect

To really surprise someone, compose a message, click the **App (A)** button, then choose **Message Effects**. You can then choose from a number of full-screen effects.

Block someone

Click on their conversation, then click **Conversations** > **Block Person...** To manage blocked contacts, open the **Preferences** window, and go to **iMessage** > **Blocked.**

Make a FaceTime video call

Make a free video call to friends and family using FaceTime...

Using the FaceTime app, you can make a video call to anyone you know that has an iPhone, iPad or Mac. As a result, you can be with friends and family at any time and any place; whether it's a birthday, anniversary, meeting, or just a quick chat.

FaceTime works over the internet, so as long as you're connected then you're good to go. Once you make or answer a call, you'll be able to enjoy crystal clear video and audio, and perhaps best of all, it's totally free to use the FaceTime app.

The basics

1 Mute your microphone using this button.

2 Turn of your video camera during a call by clicking this button.

3 Click on the **sidebar** button during a call to invite another recipient.

4 End the call by clicking on the red **X** button.

5 Make the video call fullscreen by clicking this button.

6 Take a photo of the conversation using this white button. Keep in mind that the other person will see a message to let them you've taken a photo.

Change the ringtone

If you would like to personalise your FaceTime experience with a new ringtone:

1 Click on **FaceTime** in the Finder menu bar and select **Preferences**.

1 Click the **Ringtone** drop-down, then choose a new ringtone. When you select one you'll hear a preview of it through your Mac's speakers.

Block people from calling you

If you're getting a lot of spam calls then it's possible to block people using either their email address or number. To do this:

1 Click on **FaceTime** in the Finder menu bar and select **Preferences**.

2 Click on the **Blocked** tab.

3 Click the **plus** button in the bottom left corner then enter the email addresses or phone number you wish to block.

How to set your location

1 Click on **FaceTime** in the Finder menu bar and select **Preferences**.

2 Click the **Location** dropdown.

3 Choose your preferred location.

Make a regular phone call

Yes, you can use your Mac as a giant telephone. It works by routing the call through your iPhone in the background without you knowing. To do this:

1 Select a contact using the list on the left-side of the screen, or click the **plus** button, then type a contacts name.

2 You can also type a phone number, then press the **enter** key.

3 Click the **Audio** button. Your Mac will then dial the number and make the call.

4 To end the call, just click the red button.

Take a selfie with Photo Booth

You can even apply up to 30 different visual effects...

Want to quickly take a selfie? The Photo Booth app on your Mac is the perfect way to snap a photo or even record a brief video. You can also choose from more than 30 visual effects which include mirror warp and moving imagery.

The basics

1 Use these three buttons to swap between burst mode, photo mode, and video mode.

2 Take a snapshot using this button, or press **Command-Enter** on the keyboard.

3 Explore the visual effects offered by PhotoBooth using this button.

4 Once you've taken a photo or video, click on its thumbnail to share it with others or to export it to your Mac.

Check your Stocks

Monitor the latest stocks and news, straight from your Mac...

Whether you're keeping an eye on the latest stocks, betting against them, or monitoring your portfolio, the Stocks app for macOS is a helpful way to quickly get updates on stocks and news.

Open the Stocks app, and the first thing you'll see is a sidebar listing the leading 10 stocks. To its right are the latest stock-related news stories.

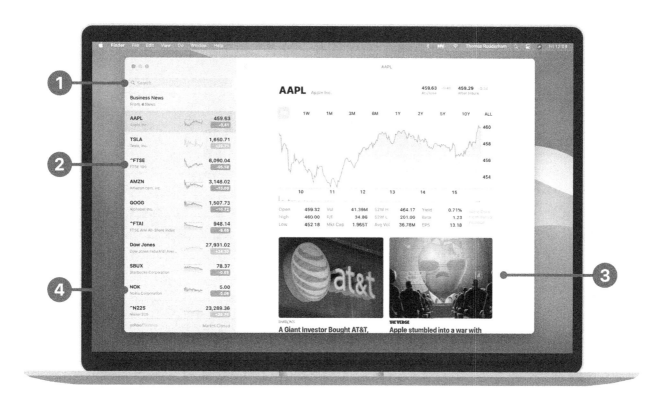

The basics

1 To add a new stock, click on the **Search** field at the top of the sidebar, then search for either the company name or its stock name.

2 Click on an individual stock and you'll see a graph of its latest performance. If it's coloured green, then the stock is generally doing well. If it's red, then it's not performing that well.

3 Click on a stock and you'll see any relevant news stories here.

4 To rearrange the Stocks in the sidebar, **click and hold** on a stock, then drag it up or down to its new position.

View and edit your Photos

Learn how to view, organise, and edit your photos...

The Photos app is a portal to your memories. Stored within its colourful icon are hundreds, if not thousands of treasured photos and videos. Photos of yapping dogs, family members, stunning landscapes, unflattering selfies and treasured holidays. This is one of those apps that you're going to be opening on a day-to-day basis, so keep it somewhere prominent on the Dock where you can quickly click it.

The basics

1 Use the slider to zoom in and out of your photos.

2 Click these 4 tabbed buttons to see your entire photo library split across days, months and years. See across the page for more.

3 Select **Search** to look for nearly anything in a photo, including both people and objects.

4 Navigate through your albums, tagged people, places, favorites, deletes images and more.

All Photos

When viewing **All Photos**, you'll see a nearly endless grid of photos scrolling upwards and off the screen. You can scroll through them and click on an image to see it bigger, or you can use the slider in the top-left corner to see your photos spread over a wider range of time.

Days

Click on the **Days** tab and you'll see a beautiful grid of images representing a single day. The Photos app intelligently organises your images, hiding duplicates while selecting a highlighted image or video.

Months

The **Months** view organises the most meaningful events into groups, then displays them as individual cards in a scrollable panel. The app tries to intelligently select the best photo or video to remind you of what the event was about. Think of it as a greatest hit library of your memories.

Years

Years gives you a high-level overview of your photo library, but what makes this view really special is it's dynamic and based on context. So open the Years view on your birthday and you'll see photos from your birthday celebrations going back as far as your photo library extends.

Search through your photos

The Photos app is incredibly intelligent. Using complex visual algorithms it can recognise objects, faces, and locations, then automatically organise images into groups. This clever form of visual recognition has another benefit: intelligent searching. It lets you search for things within an image by typing a request. To find this feature, simple click the **Search** button in the top-right corner.

Search for *"California"* and you'll see all your photos of California. Search for *"Trees"* and you'll see (you guessed it) images of trees. You can be even more specific. So search for *"Trees in California"* and the Photos app will automatically show photos of trees within California. You can try other queries such as *"Tom eating pizza"*, or *"Sarah riding a horse"* and the app will instantly present you with the correct results.

People and Places

After scanning every photo in your library to look for photos of locations and faces, the Photos app collates them into the **People and Places** section of the Photos app.

Find People and Places

To see these images just open the Photos app, then click **People** in the sidebar.

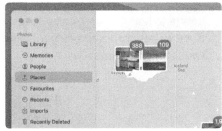

Check out the places view

Click on the **Places** link in the sidebar, and you'll see a map view with all of your photos placed in the correct location.

Watch a video of someone

To watch a video of someone in the People album, select them then click the **play** button in the bottom-right corner of their main photo.

Add a name to a person

To add a name to someone in the People album, move the cursor over their thumbnail then click the **+ Name** button.

Add someone to Favorites

If you like to regularly see the photos of a family member or friend, click on the **heart** icon to move them to the favorites area at the top of the screen.

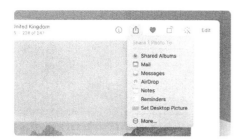

How to share a photo or video

Open an image, then click the **Share** icon in the top-right corner of the screen – it looks like a box with an arrow pointing upwards.

Select multiple images

To select multiple photos at once, click and drag the cursor over the images you wish to select. You can also hold down the **Command** key then click on multiple photos.

How to delete a photo

The easiest way is to **right-click** on the image, then choose **Delete Photo** in the pop-up window.

The basic controls of editing a photo

To improve the look of a photo, click the **Edit** button in the top-right corner, and a set of editing tools will appear:

1 Toggle between adjustment tools, filters, and the cropping tool using these tabs.

2 Rotate a photo 90 degrees using this small button at the top of the screen.

3 Click on an editing tool to access its controls. Here you can see individual sliders for adjusting the light balance of an image.

4 You can change the key image of a Live Photo by scrubbing through this timeline.

Improve an image

To automatically improve an image, click the **Wand** icon at the top of the screen. This tool analyses the image and changes its colour, contrast, and lighting to improve it.

Compare changes to a photo

If you'd like to compare your changes with the original photo at any time, click the compare button in the top-left corner of the screen.

Crop an image

Click the **Crop** tab, then either drag the edges of the image to crop it, or choose a ratio option from the sidebar on the right.

Rotate a photo

While cropping a photo, you can also rotate it. To do this, click and drag the rotate wheel to the right of the image. As it rotates you'll see a grid appear that enables you to align straight edges or an horizon.

Add a filter

The middle tab at the top of the screen enables you to add a visual filter to your image. You'll find nine to choose from, each with its own unique appearance.

Fix red eyes

If you used a flash while taking a photo, then anyone within the image might have red pupils. To fix this, click **Edit**, expand the **Red-Eye** tool, click the small brush button, then click on each red eye in the photo.

Use Retouch to remove small objects or blemishes

Photos are rarely perfect. There might be an object spoiling the view, a shadow you wish to remove, or a spot that you need to paint out. The Photos app makes it easy to fix these small errors or objects. Click **Edit**, expand the **Retouch** tool, then click on the brush icon. Next, click on the object or blemish, and the Photos app will attempt to automatically remove it.

See information about a photo

Whenever you're viewing or editing a photo, click the **info (i)** button at the top of the screen to view technical information and location-based data.

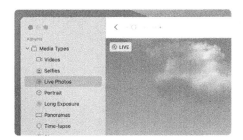

Edit Live Photos

If you've taken a photo using an iPhone or iPad, then chances are it includes a short snippet of video and audio. You'll know because a small grey button with the word **LIVE** will appear in the top-left corner of the photo. To watch the footage back, move the cursor over the **LIVE** button. You can also trim the video snippet, select a new keyframe, disable its audio, or even add a visual effect. Read on to find out how...

Select a new key frame

If you've taken an action shot and noticed that the exact moment you wanted to capture is in the moving segment of the Live Photo, then you can easily edit the photo and select the exact frame as your key photo.

To do this open the photo, click the **Edit** button, then use the timeline at the bottom of the screen to choose the new key frame. Once you've found it, click **Make Key Photo**.

Trim a Live Photo

Sometimes you might want to trim a part of the Live Photo effect. For example, maybe you suddenly moved the camera at the very last second. Whatever the reason, it's easy to trim the beginning or end.

To get started, select the photo, click **Edit**, then use the handles on either side of the timeline scrubber to fine tune the start or end points.

Create an album

It's possible to create your very own albums to better organise your photos. To do this:

1 Hover the cursor over **My Albums** in the sidebar, then click the **Plus** button.

2 Give your album a new name.

3 Click on **Photos** at the top of the screen, right-click on an image then choose **Add To** > **New Album**.

4 You can also click and drag photos into the new album in the sidebar.

Move images between albums

You can move images between albums by right-clicking on them then choosing **Add To** > **New Album**. You can also drag them from one album to another in the sidebar.

Merge albums

If you'd like to merge two albums into one, then click and drag an album in the sidebar on top of another. A pop-up window will appear asking you to confirm the merger of both albums.

Delete an album

It's easy to delete albums from your Mac. Just **right click** on them in the sidebar then choose **Delete Album**.

Listen to Music

Listen to your favorite tracks and albums on Apple Music...

The Music app is best way to listen to music on your Mac. It has a beautiful interface, offers access to millions of tracks via Apple Music, exclusive TV shows, curated playlists, videos, top charts, and even radio stations.

There's a limitless source of music available in Apple Music, but it comes at a price: to access the full service you'll need to pay a monthly subscription. It's priced slightly differently for each country, but roughly works out about the same as a takeaway pizza. For anyone who listens to the latest charts, streams music on a daily basis, or has a wide variety of music tastes, it's definitely worth the asking price. If you don't want to pay a subscription to listen to music, then you can still use Apple Music to listen to radio stations and preview music.

The basics

1 Shuffle, rewind, pause, fast forward, and loop music playback with these buttons.

2 Scrub through a song using this timeline. By clicking on the artwork thumbnail you can also minimise the Music window.

3 Click on this icon to display a right-hand sidebar with all the upcoming tracks.

4 Search both your music library and Apple Music for artists, songs and albums.

5 Click on an album to explore it, or right-click to delete it, share it, or Love/Dislike it.

6 Use this sidebar to navigate through Apple Music, your library, and any saved playlists.

 Music

Play and download 60 million songs.

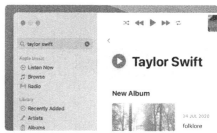

Sign up for Apple Music

Without an Apple Music subscription you can only listen to 30-second preview clips. You can sign up for a monthly subscription through the Music app by clicking the **Listen Now** option in the sidebar.

Explore Apple Music

Once subscribed, you'll find literally millions of tracks, albums, playlists, radio stations, and music videos within Apple Music. Click on the **Browse** button in the sidebar to explore it.

Search for music

If you're looking for an artist, song, album, or even lyrics, then click the **Search** bar in the sidebar. You can use the two tabs in the top-right corner to search through either Apple Music or your library.

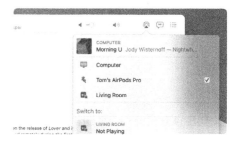

Add music to your Library

If there's a track or album that you'd like to save to your Library, click the **+Add** button at the top of the screen.

Download new music

To automatically download music to your Mac whenever you add a new album or track, click on **Music** in the Apple menu, choose **Preferences**, then tick **Automatic Downloads**.

Stream music to your AirPods

To listen to music over your AirPods, Bluetooth headphones, or an Apple TV, click on the **AirPlay** button next to the volume slider, then choose a device.

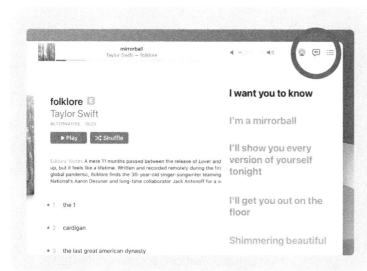

View music lyrics

Have you ever struggled to understand the lyrics of a song as it plays in the background? Using the Music app you can see lyrics for all your favourite songs, and they update in realtime so you can follow along. Think of it as your own karaoke machine. Here's how it works:

When listening to a song, click on the **lyrics** button in the top-right corner of the screen. It looks like a small speech bubble. You'll then see a lyrics sidebar appear on the right-side of the screen.

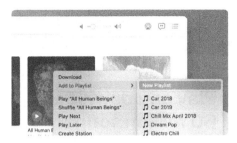

Shuffle music

If you're bored of an albums track order, click **Shuffle** and you'll never know what song is coming up next.

Create a Playlist

Think of a playlist as a custom-made album. To create a playlist of your own, click on **File** in the menu, choose **New**, then **Playlist**. You can then give it a name.

Add to an existing playlist

To add a track or album to the new playlist, **right-click** on the track then choose **Add to a Playlist...**

Delete a track or album

Fed up with a song or album? Just **right-click** on the track name or album artwork, then click **Delete from Library**.

Like music to improve your recommendations list

Whenever you hear a great track or album, **right-click** on the music then choose **Love**. This tells Apple Music what genre and style of music you like. Keep doing this and over time the For You playlists and recommendations will get more and more accurate to your tastes in music.

Display the Mini Player

The Music app takes up a lot of space across the screen, but helpfully there's a miniature version that's easier to manage. To display it:

1. Click on **Window** in the Apple menu at the top of the screen, then click **Mini Player**.

2. You can now minise the main window by pressing **Command-M**.

3. To close the Mini Player, click the **red button** in the top-left corner.

Create a station of music

If you're listening to an album or track and want to listen to similar music, then your Mac can automatically look for similar tracks and albums, then turn them into an endless radio station. Here's how it works:

1. While listening to music, click on the **options** button at the top of the screen.

2. Click on **Create Station**. Your Mac will then start playing an endless stream of similar music.

Share your music with everyone on Apple Music

When you open the Music app for the first time, you'll be asked if you would like to share your music with friends and family. You can click **Get Started** to set this feature up straight away, but if you'd like to do it later then click **Listen Now** in the sidebar, click your **user icon** in the top-right corner, then click the **Edit** to the right of your name. Here's how it works:

1 Start by choosing a profile photo and user name, then decide if anyone can follow you, or just those you approve.

2 Choose if you would like to show your custom playlists within your profile or in search on Apple Music.

3 To let people see what you're listening too in realtime, click on the small piece of blue text that says **Additional Privacy Settings**, then toggle **Listening To** on.

4 Click the blue **Done** button to save the changes. People can now find you by searching for your username in Apple Music

Radio stations

Click **Radio** in the sidebar to listen to Apple Music 1, radio stations from around the country, plus bespoke stations that are automatically compiled around your listening history.

Check out music videos

To browse the latest music videos, click on **Browse** in the sidebar, scroll down to the bottom of the screen, then click **Music Videos**.

See the top charts

What to see what's number one in the charts? Click on **Browse** in the sidebar, scroll down to the bottom of the screen, then click **Top Charts**.

Watch TV & Movies

Never miss an episode of your favorite show with this helpful app...

With so many sources of video content, subscription services, and streaming neworks, it has become difficult to keep track of the latest episodes of your favorite TV shows. Thankfully, the Apple TV app for the Mac makes it a little bit easier, by collating many of the latest releases into one app. It also houses any TV shows or movies which you've purchased on iTunes, enables you to stream videos to your Apple TV, and remembers where you last left off.

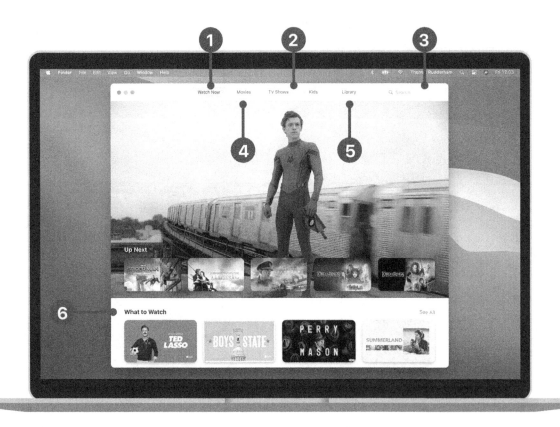

The basics

1 If you're looking for inspiration, click **Watch Now** to find suggested TV shows and movies.

2 Click the **Kids** tab to find a wide range of content suitable for children.

3 It's pretty obvious, but by clicking **Search** you can look for movies, TV shows, or cast.

4 Explore the very latest film rentals and purchases by clicking on **Movies**.

5 You'll find all of your purchases in the **Library** section of the app, split into TV Shows and Movies.

6 Quickly jump between suggested movies, TV, or kids shows with these helpful shortcuts.

Learn more about cast or crew

Search for an actor, producer, director, or other member of crew, and you can see what films they've been in, worked upon, or made a guest appearance within.

Find the top rentals

From the **Watch Now** area, scroll down until you find the **More to Explore** panel. Scroll to the left and you'll find a shortcut to the most popular movie rentals.

See what's on Apple TV+

Apple TV+ promises to be a serious competitor to Netflix and Amazon Prime. You can see what's available and coming soon by clicking **Apple TV+**, then browsing its content.

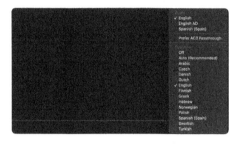

Audio sources and subtitles

While watching a video, click the **speech** icon next to the playback timer to toggle different audio sources or subtitles.

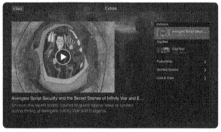

Access movie special features

If you've rented or purchased a movie with special features, then you can access these by clicking the **Extras** button in the bottom-right corner of the screen.

Jump between chapters

Click on the **Chapters** button in the bottom-right corner to skip through a movie. You can also move the cursor to the top of the screen and use the Chapters menu option too.

Turn on Home Sharing

You can use your Mac to stream videos to an Apple TV, iPhone, or iPad, by turning on Home Sharing. To do this open the **System Preferences** app, click **Sharing**, select **Media Sharing**, then toggle **Home Sharing** on.

Stream to your Apple TV

To play media from your Mac on an Apple TV, open the **Computers** app on the Apple TV, then look for the **Library** option.

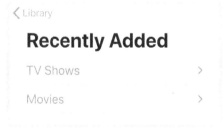

Stream to your iPhone or iPad

To play movies stored on your Mac on an iPhone or iPad, open the **TV** app on either device, tap **Library**, then select *My Name* **Library**.

Watch videos with QuickTime

A helpful tool for watching and trimming local video files on your Mac...

Installed on your Mac is a helpful little app called QuickTime Player. It's the default video player for files you might download from the internet, but it can also be used to play audio files, crop videos or record your Mac's display in its entirety.

Play a video

Double click on a video file and it will open in QuickTime Player. Press the spacebar key to begin playing the video, or move the cursor over it to access controls which enable you to play, pause, adjust the volume, scrub along the timeline and share the video.

Fast forward or rewind

Hover over a video to access its controls, then click on the forward/back arrows and you'll play the video back at double-speed. If you triple-click the arrows you'll play the video back at 5x speed, click 4 times for 10x playback speed.

Go frame-by-frame

If you want to study a video in detail, simply press the left or right arrow keys on your keyboard and you'll be able to scrub through the video one frame at a time. Hold down an arrow key and the video will play back at half speed.

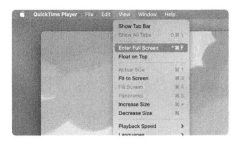

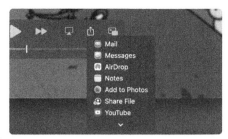

Watch a video full screen

If you really want to settle down and enjoy a video, press **Command-F** to play it back full screen. You can also go to **View** > **Enter Full Screen** to perform the same command.

Resize the video window

If you want to adjust the size of the video playback window simply move your cursor to the corner of the video, then click and drag it. You'll see the video window change in size as it follows the cursor.

Share a video

Click the **Share** icon to the right of the playback controls (it looks like a square with an arrow pointing upwards out of it). You'll see the share panel appear as a pop-up window, with icons and shortcuts to each sharing ability.

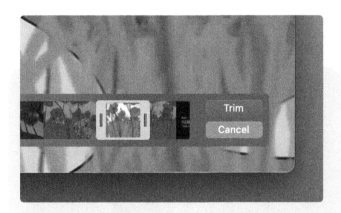

Trim a video

You might not know it, but QuickTime Player supports basic video editing tools, enabling you to trim a video then re-save it in various formats. Here's how it works:

1. While viewing a video, press **Command-T** to access the trim tools.

2. Drag the yellow handles to trim the video to its new length.

3. Click the **Trim** button to save your changes.

Export a video at a different size

If you would like to save a video in a different size, say one suited perfectly for a 1080p television, then QuickTime Player offers a set of export controls for doing just this. You'll find five options: 4K, 1080p, 720p, 480p, and Audio only. Here's how to export a video from QuickTime Player:

1. Open a video in QuickTime Player, then go to **File** > **Export As** and choose a size.

2. Give the video a suitable name and pick a save location.

3. Click **Save** and wait for QuickTime Player to export the video.

Use Maps to explore the world

Discover new places, get route guidance, and more...

With a map of the entire globe on your Mac, it's now possible to explore every inch of the world. That's exactly what the Maps app gives you, alongside directions, real-time traffic information, transit timetables, 3D views of major cities and more.

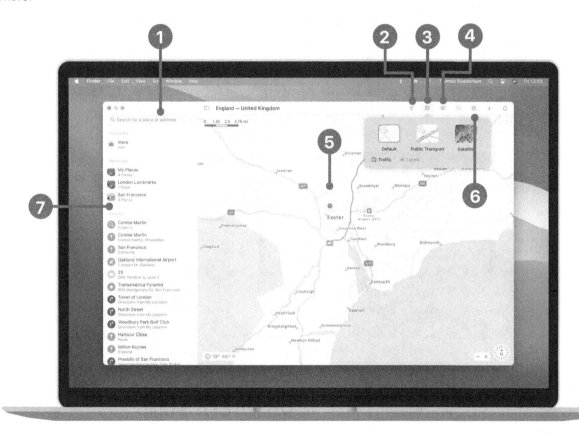

The basics

1 Click on the **search field** to search for a place, address, or landmark.

2 Click on this **arrow** icon to move the maps view to your current location.

3 Click on the **view** button to choose from three different views of the world: Default, Public Transport, and Satellite.

4 Click the **3D** button to tilt the camera upwards slightly.

5 This blue dot represents your current location in the world.

6 Click the **directions** button to get route guidance from one location to another.

6 The sidebar automatically displays your recent activity. You'll also find any collections of places you've saved alongside recently viewed locations.

See a 3D map

Using the Maps app it's possible to navigate the world's most famous cities in beautiful 3D graphics. To do this, ensure you're in **satellite** mode then zoom in on the map. When you're close to the ground, you'll notice a **3D** button appear in the upper-right corner. Click it and the Maps view will tilt, then load a 3D landscape with detailed 3D buildings.

- To rotate the image, place two fingers on the trackpad then rotate them, or hold down the **option** key then move the mouse left or right.
- To tilt the camera, simultaneously move two fingers up or down the trackpad, or hold down the **option** key and move the mouse up or down.

Take a Look Around in first-person

Chances are you've seen Google's Street View. It's a great piece of technology that lets you explore the world at street level using 360-degree imagery. Apple's Look Around mode is similar, but it's more polished, realistic, and includes tags that you can click on to explore businesses and landmarks.

To use the Look Around mode, zoom the map until you see a binocular icon appear in the top-right corner. At the time of writing, it will only appear in major cities within the United States. Once you see it, click the **binocular** icon, and the map view will zoom down to street level.

- To pan the view, click and drag the cursor around the screen. To move in any direction, double-click where you want to go. You can also click on a tag to see more information about the place or business.
- One last tip: click the **minimise** icon in the top-left corner to shrink the Look Around view and place it above the 2D map. You can now click on a new location on the map, and the Look Around view will update to show you street-level imagery.

Enjoy a flyover tour

Want to explore a city like never before? Simply search for the city's name then click the **Flyover Tour** button in the information panel. You will then be treated to a 3D tour of the city.

Search indoor maps with "Look Inside"

With the Maps app you can find your way around airports and shopping centres using the indoor maps feature, which displays the locations of stores, toilets, and more. Most international airports and major shopping centres are fully mapped. Just look for a "Look Inside" badge that appears beneath the name of the airport. When you see it, click **Look Inside** and you'll see a detailed interior map of the location.

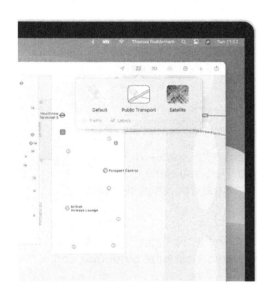

See Transit information

If you're exploring a location using public transport then it's a good idea to view the local area using the **Transit** view. This lets you see nearby train stations, tube lines, bus stations, taxi pick-up points, and more. To enable this view simply click the **views** icon at the top of the screen, then choose **Public Transport**.

Drop a pin to find out more

To see detailed information about a specific point, zoom into that spot, click **Edit** in the Apple menu, then choose **Drop Pin**. A pin will then fall on the map and display information about the location, alongside directions.

Share a location

Want to send an address to friends and family? Just search for the location then click the **Share** icon in the top corner of the screen.

Search Maps using Siri

If you'd rather search for a place or person using Siri, click the **Siri** icon in the Finder menu then say something like "*where is the nearest hotel?*".

Turn-by-turn navigation

Your Mac can't be used as a sat-nav device, but it can plan directions for you and offer multiple routes.

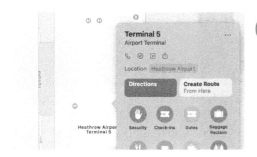

1 To get started, open Maps then click the **Search** field at the top of the window. Next, enter the destination you wish the navigate too. This can be an address, post/zip code, or landmark.

2 Once you've searched for an address a pop-up window will appear showing details for the location. Click the blue **Directions** button, and Maps will automatically find the optimal route to the destination. It will also offer alternative routes, if any are available, which appear as opaque blue lines on the map. You can click on these alternative routes to choose them.

3 Once you've found a suitable route tap, click the **small arrow** button in the directions suggestions panel, and you'll see an overview of the entire journey.

Add a scale to the map

If you need a better idea of distances and scale, click **View** in the Finder menu then select **Show Scale**. In the upper-left corner of the map you will now see a scale (in either km or miles).

Walking or cycling directions

If you're planning a route on foot or a bike, then use the small graphical buttons to select either walking or cycling directions. If going by bike, then you can plan a route that avoids hills and busy roads.

Report an issue with the map

To report an error or missing place, click **Maps** in the Apple menu, then choose **Report an Issue...**

Create Reminders

Set yourself reminders so you'll never forget a thing...

Your Mac already includes a notes app that can be used to jot down ideas and thoughts, but Reminders makes it easy to create to-do lists, set deadlines, and organise your life. It can also remind you with alerts at pre-determined times.

That's not all the app does, of course. It can group reminders into categories and even sync reminders across all your Apple devices via iCloud.

The basics

1 Search for reminders, lists, or list items using the search bar at the top of the screen.

2 Select a reminder or list here. You can also rearrange items by clicking, holding, then dragging.

3 You can add additional items to a reminder list by clicking in the white space beneath an item.

4 To create a brand new reminder list, click the **Add List** button in the bottom-left corner.

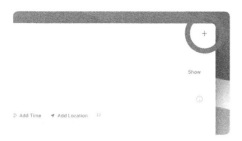

Create a new Reminder

Click the **Reminders** option in the sidebar, then click the **Plus** icon in the very top-right corner. This will create a new reminder in the main panel.

Remind at a date and time

To remind yourself to do something at a specific date and time, click on the new reminder, then click the **i** button. On the next panel, click **Remind me on a day**, then set a day and specific time if necessary.

Remind yourself at a location

Similarly, you can also remind yourself when you reach a location. To do this click the **Remind me at a location** button, then either enter an address or choose from one of the suggested options.

Share a reminder

To share a reminder with someone, move the cursor over the Reminder in the sidebar then click the small **avatar** icon which appears. You'll then see a share panel appear.

Create a folder of reminders

You can create folders of reminders by dragging one on top of the other in the sidebar. You'll then be able to give the new folder a name.

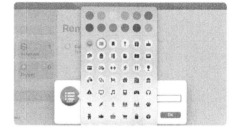

Assign a colour and icon

Right-click on a reminder or list in the sidebar then click **Show Info**. In the pop-up window you'll be able to re-name the reminder. Move the cursor over the icon and you can also assign a colour and icon.

Delete reminders

To delete a reminder or list in the sidebar, **right-click** on it then choose **Delete** in the pop-up window.

Create a reminder using Siri

You can also add reminders by using Siri. Just click the **Siri** icon in the top corner of the Finder menu, then say something like "*Remind me to pick up Sam*". Siri will then automatically create a new reminder.

115

Create, edit, and share Notes

Learn how to quickly jot down notes, plus much more...

At first glance, the Notes app is a fairly basic way to jot down ideas and lists. It's much more than that, however. With the Notes app you can collaborate with friends, draw and annotate, scan documents, format text, create tables and more.

The basics

1 You can view your notes as thumbnail images (rather than a list view) by clicking this icon.

2 To delete a note, select it first then click this **Trash** icon.

3 Create a table within a note by clicking this icon.

4 Share, print, or save a note by clicking the **Share** button.

5 Search through your notes by entering a keyword into the search field.

6 You can jump between different Note accounts and folders by using this sidebar.

Create a new note

To create a new Note, open the **Notes** app then click the **New Note** button in the upper-left corner. You can also press **Command-N** on the keyboard.

Sketch a note

You can use your iPhone or iPad to add a sketch into a note. To do this click the **Photo** button at the top of the screen, choose **Add Sketch**, then select your iPhone or iPad.

Change the line colour

While drawing a sketch on your iPhone or iPad, you can change the colour of the line by tapping one of the coloured dots along the bottom of the screen. Tap on the multicoloured circle to access additional colours.

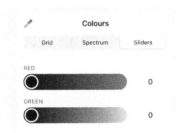

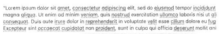

Alter the brush thickness

Double-tap on a drawing tool and you'll be able to adjust its thickness and opacity.

Insert a photo

Click the **Photo** button at the top of the screen, then choose **Photos...** You can also drag and drop an image from the Finder onto the note.

Format text

To format text or add a numbered/bulleted list, click the small **Aa** button at the top of the screen, then choose an option.

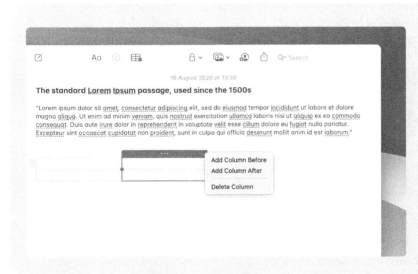

Create a table

It's surprisingly easy to create a simple table and embed it into a note. Start by creating or opening a note, click where you want to insert the table then click the **Table** button at the top of the screen. You'll then see a 2-by-2 table appear within the note.

You can add content to a row or column by clicking the appropriate area, or add additional rows and columns by clicking the buttons above or to the left of the table.

Share a note

Want to send a note to someone else? Just click the **Share** button and you'll see options for emailing the note, sending it to another device via AirDrop, or copying it.

Print a note

Press **Command-P** on your keyboard, or click **File** in the Finder menu, then choose **Print**.

Delete a note

While viewing the notes list, swipe across the note you wish to remove from right to left, or right-click and choose **Delete**.

Collaborate on a note

If you'd like to share and collaborate on a note with friends and family then it's an easy process. If you're the creator of the note then it's yours to share, meaning you can invite others, see changes happen in real-time, and remove access to anyone that you've invited. Here's how it works:

1 Select the note that you would like to share, then click the **Collaborate** button at the top of the screen.

2 Use the Share panel to invite others from your Contacts book. You can also send invites via Message, Mail, Twitter and more.

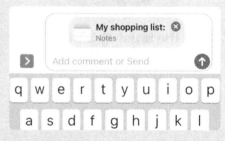

3 Anyone invited will receive an iCloud link to open your note. If they're using a Mac or iOS device, then they can use the link to access the note.

4 To remove someone's permission, click the **Collaborate** button, click the **options** button next to the person's name, then choose **Remove Access**.

5 If you're tired of seeing notifications every time someone makes a change, click the **Collaborate** button, then un-toggle **Highlight All Changes**.

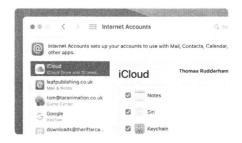

Lock a note

To prevent anyone with access to your Mac from reading a note, **right-click** on it in the sidebar, choose **Lock Note**, then enter a password. You'll need to enter this each time you open the note.

Change the default text size

If you find the default text size too small (or too big), then click **File** in the Finder Menu, choose **Preferences**, then use the **Default text size** slider to adjust text size.

Change the default account

If you have multiple internet accounts set up on your Mac, then you can toggle Notes on or off for each by going to **System Preferences** > **Internet Accounts**.

Scan a document

If you have an iPhone to hand, then it's possible to scan letters and documents and attach them directly to a note on your Mac. What's great is that scans actually look like scanned documents, thanks to some clever post-processing which straightens the image and fixes any white balance issues. To scan a document:

1 Start by clicking the photos button in the top corner, then choose **Scan Documents**.

2 The camera on your iPhone will automatically open.

3 Move the camera view over the document you wish to scan and your iPhone will automatically recognise it.

4 Tap **Keep Scan** to save the image. You can continue to scan further documents, or tap **Save** to attach the image/s to your notes.

5 The scan will now be attached to your note as an image.

An overview of System Preferences

Get to know the basics of the System Preferences app...

Whenever you want to make a change to your Mac, adjust a setting, or add a new piece of hardware (such as a printer), then System Preferences is the place to go. You can access System Preferences at any time by:

1. Clicking the **Apple** logo in the Finder menu, then **System Preferences**.
2. Clicking the **System Preferences** icon in the Dock.
3. Opening the **Launchpad**, then clicking **System Preferences**.

Once you open the System Preferences app you'll see a grid of shortcut icons. They're labelled logically, so if you want to add another user account to your Mac, then click Users & Groups; and if you want to change the background wallpaper choose Desktop & Screen Saver.

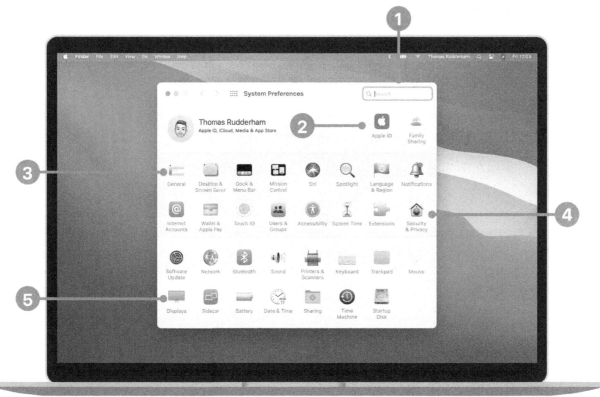

The basics

1 If there's a particular setting that you're trying to find, use the **search** field to quickly locate it.

2 Click **Apple ID** to edit your personal details, password and security settings, and iCloud settings.

3 Click on **General** to toggle Dark Mode on or off, or adjust the basic colour scheme.

4 You can change your password, open apps from outside of the App Store, and access an entire suite of privacy settings from here.

5 Adjust the brightness, resolution, colour profile, and Night Shift settings from here.

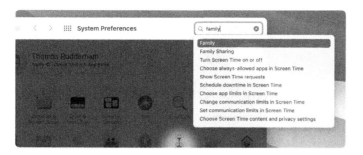

Search through Settings

If you're not sure where a particular setting is, then you can quickly search for it using the **Search** box in the top-right corner. As you type, System Preferences will attempt to guess what you're looking for, then use a spotlight to show you where to go.

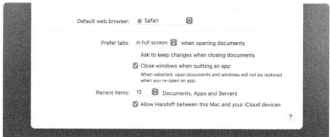

Change the default web browser

If you have more than one web browser installed on your Mac, then here's how to change the default app: open the **System Preferences** app, click **General**, then use the **Default web browser** drop-down to select another app.

Adjust the date, time, or temperature format

To quickly toggle between locations, date and time formats, temperature formats, and calendar formats, open **System Preferences** and click on the **Language & Region** option in the upper-right corner.

Explore the Battery panel

It's a good idea to put it your Mac to sleep whenever you're not using it, but if you prefer to leave it on all the time, or adjust how your Mac manages efficiency while running on battery power, open the **System Preferences app**, click **Battery**, then click the **Battery** option in the sidebar.

Enable voice dictation

If you'd like to talk to your Mac to dictate text, open **System Preferences**, select **Keyboard**, then click the **Dictation** tab. You'll then see an option to turn voice dictation on and use it wherever you can type text.

Check for system updates

If you want to see if a new update is available for your Mac then go to **System Preferences** > **Software Update**. On the following panel you can download and install updates, or toggle Automatic Updates on, which lets your Mac automatically download and install new updates overnight.

Users & Groups

Learn how to create separate accounts for the people who use your Mac...

If your Mac is the main computer at home, then it's likely that at some point another member of your household is going to use it. Maybe they want to quickly print something, or perhaps they want to use it to work for a few hours; whatever the reason, it's probably a good idea to set up a separate account for them.

By creating separate user accounts, you can let each person personalise settings, save their own passwords, install apps, and modify options without affecting anyone else. You can also create groups of users to share privileges between multiple people.

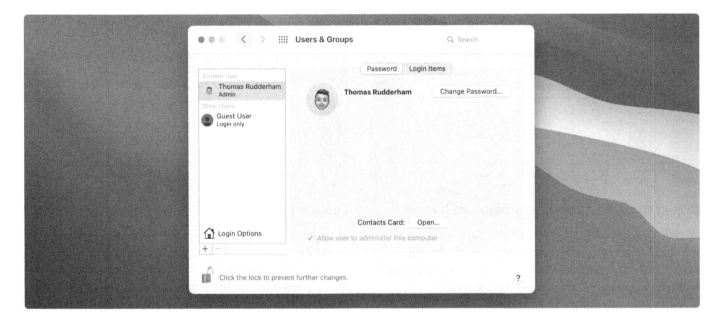

Add a new user

1 Open the **System Preferences** app, then click on **Users & Groups**.

2 Click the **padlock** icon, and enter the administrator username and password.

3 Click the **plus** button underneath the list of users.

4 In the New Account pop-up menu, choose a type of user. Here's a quick overview of what each does:

- **Administrator**: An administrator can add and manage other users on your Mac, install new apps, and change any setting. Your Mac can have multiple administrators, and you can convert them to regular users at any time.
- **Standard**: Standard users are created by administrators. They can also install new apps and change their own settings, but can't add other users.
- **Sharing Only**: The most limited type of account, Sharing Only users can only see files shared to the Mac remotely, and can't change settings on the Mac.

Automatically log into your Mac

If you don't want to enter your password every time you turn on your Mac, then it's possible to skip the login screen entirely. This saves time, but it's worth noting that anyone who turns on your Mac can also log in and access your files. If you're sure that no one else will ever have access to your Mac, then you can turn on automatic login by:

1 From **Users & Groups**, click the **Login Options** button underneath the list of users.

2 Click on the **Automatic Login** dropdown, then select the appropriate user from the dropdown list.

Add a new group

By creating a group of users, you can easily share privileges between multiple people. For example, you can create a rule that lets a group of users share access to the same folder, or limit a group from installing any third-party apps. Here's how it works:

1 From **Users & Groups**, click the **Add** button underneath the list of users.

2 In the **New Account** pop-up menu, select **Group**.

3 Give the group a name, then click **Create Group**.

4 A new window will appear, enabling you to assign users to the new Group. Once you've added everyone, just close the System Preferences window to save the changes.

Create a guest account

There are many reasons to let guests use your computer. It saves you having to create separate accounts for relatives and friends, it prevents anyone using your Mac from seeing your files and settings, and you can assign limitations to guest accounts to prevent people from doing things that they shouldn't. Also, anything a guest user saves or downloads is saved to a temporary location, then automatically deleted when they log out.

How's how to activate the guest account feature:

1 From **Users & Groups**, click on the **Guest User** account.

2 Click the checkbox next to **Allow guest to log into the computer**.

That's it. Guests can now use your Mac. To assign limitations using the Parental Control window, turn over the page.

Family Sharing

Let the entire family share media, purchases, and even games...

With Family Sharing enabled on your Mac, it's possible for up to six family members to share content and purchases across iTunes, Apple Music, Apple Books, the App Store, Apple News+, and Apple TV. One adult in the household needs to act as the administrator. They can invite other family members, choose features, and approve purchases; while the rest of the family enjoys shared music, photos and more.

Basic features:

- **Share purchases.** Once an app, TV show, movie or book is purchased, it's instantly available to everyone else too.

- **Apple Music.** Unlimited music for the entire family with a family membership plan.

- **iCloud storage.** One plan to store everyone's photos, files, and backups.

- **Location Sharing.** Everyone in the family can share their location via the Messages app or Find My Friends. They can also track each other's devices.

- **Apple TV content.** The whole family can access the latest Apple TV shows across all of their devices.

- **Apple Arcade subscription.** Let everyone in the family play the latest games in Apple Arcade.

- **Apple News+.** Get the latest magazines and exclusive news stories.

Set up Family Sharing

The adult in the family is the one who should set up Family Sharing. If they enable purchase sharing then they will be asked to verify that they agree to pay for purchases initiated by family members, and that they have a valid payment method on file. With that in mind, the next step is to:

1 Open **System Preferences**, then click on **Family Sharing**.

2 Follow the on-screen prompts to enable Family Sharing. You'll be asked whether you'd like to share music, movies, TV shows, apps and books purchased with your Apple ID. You'll also be asked if you'd like to pay for purchases made by other members of your family.

How to invite a family member

Whenever you want to add a family member:

1 Open **System Preferences**, then click on **Family Sharing**.

2 Click **Add family member....**

3 Enter your family member's name, email address, or Game Centre nickname.

If they're with you they can enter their Apple ID address and password and be added straight away. Otherwise, an invitation will be sent on your behalf. Once they have accepted they will appear in the Family Members sidebar.

Enable Purchase Sharing

With Purchase Sharing enabled, you can buy something from iTunes, iBooks, or the App Store, then everyone in your family can download it for free too. To turn Purchase Sharing on:

1 Open **System Preferences**, then click on **Family Sharing**.

2 Click **Purchase Sharing** in the sidebar.

3 Click the **My Apps & Services** tab.

4 Click the **Share my purchases** checkbox.

You can manage the shared payment method from this panel, or disable Purchase Sharing at a later date.

Restrict content using Screen Time

Make sure your kids don't access anything inappropriate...

Letting your kid's roam free on the internet is a scary idea. Thankfully, you don't have to look over their shoulder all the time, because the Content Privacy Restrictions panel in Screen Time lets you protect them while they browse the web. It's possible to block adult websites, explicit content, set time limits, and monitor what they access.

Turn on Content & Privacy Restrictions

To restrict content, you'll first need a separate user account for your kid's. Once created, you can begin setting restrictions and time limits. Here's how it works:

1. Log into the account you wish to restrict, then open **System Preferences**.

2. Next, click on **Screen Time**. Look for the **Content & Privacy** option at the bottom of the sidebar. Click it, then click **Turn On...** in the upper-right corner.

3. Most of the options are fairly self explanatory, so to restrict adult websites, click **Limit Adult Websites**.

4. To create a custom list of approved websites, click **Allowed Websites Only**, then click **Customise**... to add and edit a pre-populated list of child-friendly websites.

5. Click the **Stores** tab and you'll find options for blocking explicit books, films, TV shows, and apps.

6. Click the **Apps** tab and you can prevent children from opening built-in apps, enabling the camera, or using Siri.

7. Click the **Other** tab and you'll find options for preventing a child from making passcode changes, account changes, and even using mobile data.

View an activity report of your Mac usage

Using the Screen Time panel it's possible to view daily or weekly reports of your Mac usage. You can see how long you've spent using apps, how many notifications you've received, and even how many times you've opened apps (Apple calls this "Pickups").

1 Open the **System Preferences** app, then click on **Screen Time.** At the top of the panel you should see a brief report on how long you've spent using apps on your Mac.

2 Click the **Categories** button below the graph and you'll see a brief overview of the total time spent on your Mac, broken down into categories.

3 To see how long you've spent using apps over the course of a week, click on the date in the upper-right corner, then choose **This Week**.

4 Click on **Notifications** in the sidebar to see which apps have been sending you the most notifications.

5 Click **Pickups** in the sidebar, and you'll see how many times you've opened apps.

Other things you can restrict using Screen Time

By navigating through the sidebar in the Screen Time panel, you'll find options for limiting apps, or blocking a massive amount of content and features, including:

- App installation
- Location Sharing
- Changes to passcodes
- Account changes
- Mobile data limits
- Volume limit

- Explicit language
- Screen recording
- Multiplayer games
- Explicit entertainment and books

Security

Keep your data, apps, and personal details secure...

Your Mac contains personal information, treasured photos, contact details, payment details, messages, and more, so it's incredibly important to protect it with the right types and levels of security.

The basics

The first place you should visit is the **Security & Privacy** panel in the **System Preferences** app. Once there you'll see four tab shortcuts for accessing the following security settings: General, FileVault, Firewall, and Privacy. To make any changes, click the **padlock** icon in the bottom-left corner, then enter your account password.

Change your password

Click the **Change Password** button within the **General** panel. In the slide-down panel, enter your old password, your new password, then a subtle password hint.

Require a password after putting the Mac to sleep

By default, your Mac will ask for your password immediately after it has gone to sleep, or after the screen saver begins. To change this from anywhere between five seconds and eight hours, look for the **Require password** drop-down, then use it to select a period of time.

Privacy Settings

The **Privacy** tab in the Security & Privacy panel lets you monitor and control a number of different settings:

- **Location Services.** From here you can prevent apps and services from accessing your location.

- **Contacts, Calendar and Reminders.** From these three panels you can prevent apps from accessing your personal data.

- **Photos.** Click on this panel to see which apps have requested access to your photo library.

- **Accessibility.** You can't control accessibility settings from here. Instead, you can see which apps are able to control your Mac using accessibility features.

- **Analytics**. From this panel you can share data with Apple and app developers, such as how you use their apps or any crash log data.

Turn on the Firewall

A Firewall works by constantly monitoring your Mac's network connection, then blocking any unwanted traffic coming in or out of your machine. It's a good idea to have it running all the time to ensure your Mac stays safe from potential threats. To do this:

1 Click the **Firewall** tab within the **Security & Privacy** panel, then click the **padlock** icon in the lower-left corner and enter your account password.

2 Click **Turn On Firewall.**

3 Click the **Firewall Options** button and, in the dialog box that appears, click the **Enable Stealth Mode** checkbox. This will make your Mac invisible on public networks, such as shared Wi-Fi in a cafe.

Keep in mind that a Firewall will only protect you from threats on the web. It can't prevent local attacks, which typically happens when a rougue app is installed locally on your Mac.

Use FileVault to protect all your files

If you use your Mac for data-sensitive tasks, or want to prevent anyone from ever accessing your files (such as in a theft), then you might want to use FileVault to protect your files. It works by encrypting all of the data on your Mac with XTS-AES-128 encryption and a 256-bit key. When enabled, you will be asked to enter your password every time your Mac is powered on. To turn FileVault on:

1 Click the **FileVault** tab.

2 Click the **padlock** icon in the lower-left corner and enter your account password.

3 Click **Turn On FileVault**.

If there are multiple accounts on your Mac then you'll see a message asking for each user to type their password before they will be able to unlock the hard drive. User accounts that you add after enabling FileVault are automatically enabled.

Click **Continue**, then select how you would like to unlock your disk in case you ever forget your password. You can choose to do this using your Apple ID and password, or with a recovery key and three personal questions.

Notes about FileVault:

- Your files and startup disk are encrypted in the background as you use your Mac, and only when your Mac is awake and plugged into a power source.

- Any new files that you create are automatically encrypted.

- When FileVault set up is complete and you restart your Mac, you will need to enter your account password to unlock your disk.

- FileVault requires that you log into your Mac every time it starts up.

- No account is permitted to log in automatically.

A guide to accessibility settings

Enable visual, audio, and physical accommodations...

Your Mac might be an intuitive computer to use, but it's also packed with assistive features to help those with visual impairments or motor control limitations. You'll find the majority of them in the Accessibility panel within the System Preferences app. To get there, open **System Preferences**, then select **Accessibility**.

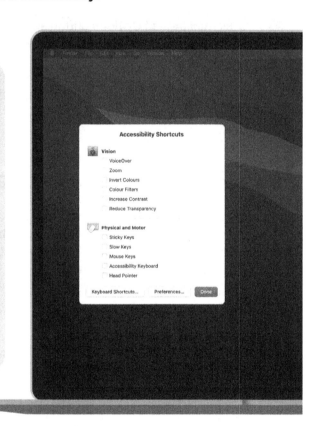

Quickly access options

By default, you can access common accessibility options at any time by pressing **Option**, **Command**, and **F5**.

From this panel you can quickly turn on accessibility features such as Voice Over, Sticky Keys, and Screen Zoom. Alternatively, to add an accessibility shortcut to the menu bar:

1. Open the **System Preferences** app.

2. Select **Accessibility**.

3. Click **Show Accessibility status in menu bar.**

Make the cursor bigger

If you're struggling to see the cursor there are two things you can do. First, try shaking the mouse or shaking your finger on the trackpad. You'll see the cursor jiggle and get bigger for a moment. Second, you can actually make the cursor bigger. To do this:

1. Open the **System Preferences** app, then click **Accessibility**.

2. Click **Display** in the sidebar, click the **Cursor** tab, then use the **Cursor size** slider to increase the cursor size.

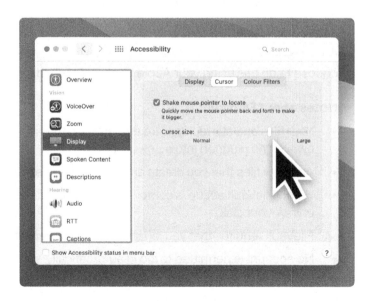

Invert the colours of your screen

For those with a sensitivity to brightness, macOS includes an accessibility feature that inverts every colour of the screen. Cleverly, media content like photos and videos *are not* inverted. To turn it on:

1 Open the **System Preferences** app, then click **Accessibility**.

2 Click **Display** in the sidebar, then click **Invert colours.**

3 You'll instantly see your Mac's screen invert. If you don't find this option helpful, then you can deactivate it by clicking **Invert colours** again.

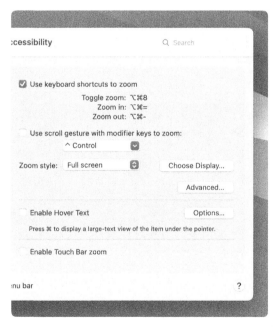

Zoom the screen

There might be occasions where you need to zoom the entire screen. Perhaps the text on a website is too small, or you can't quite make out the detail on an image. Those with visual impairments might also appreciate the ability to zoom the entire screen. Thankfully, using a keyboard shortcut it's easy to zoom in and out. To do this:

1 Open the **System Preferences** app, select **Accessibility**, then click **Zoom** in the sidebar.

2 Click **Use keyboard shortcuts to zoom**.

To zoom in, press **Option > Command > =** on your keyboard. To zoom out, press **Option > Command > -**

To pan the screen, simply move the cursor to the edge of the screen and it will follow the cursor.

Use a magnifying glass

If you would rather zoom into a small area, rather than the entire screen, go to the **Accessibility** panel, click **Zoom** in the sidebar, then use the **Zoom style** drop-down to select **Picture-in-picture**.

Now, when you zoom using **Option > Command > =**, you'll see a small rectangle appear, with the content beneath zoomed in. This rectangle will follow the cursor, so you can get a closer look at things by simply moving the cursor over it.

macOS Updates

Make sure you've always got the latest system updates installed...

Keeping your Mac up to date with the latest software releases is the best way to prevent security threats, fix software bugs, and get access to the latest features. Your Mac will always remind you when there are updates available via a notification alert in the top-right corner of the screen, but it's easy to manually check for updates, or schedule updates to install when you're away from the computer.

Manually check for updates

To check whether a software update is available for your Mac:

1 Open the **System Preferences** app, then click **Software Update** in the lower-left corner.

2 Your Mac will check with Apple to see if any updates are available.

3 If so, then you'll see the version number and a brief summary. To install the update, click **Update Now**.

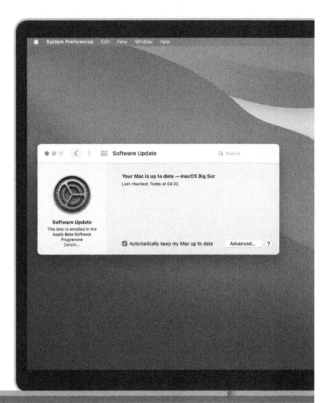

Check out the Advanced settings panel

While looking at the Software Update panel, click the **Advanced** button in the bottom-right corner to find a selection of additional settings:

- **Check for updates.** Tick this to let your Mac automatically look for updates.
- **Download new updates when available.** Un-tick this if you don't want to download updates in the background.
- **Install macOS updates.** Un-tick this if you want to install updates when you're ready to, rather than straight away.
- **Install app updates from the App Store.** Un-tick this if you don't want your apps to automatically update in the background.
- **Install system data files and security updates.** Un-tick this to prevent security updates from being installed automatically. This might be important if you use your Mac in a corporate environment.

To check and install app updates

If you're looking to update the apps on your Mac, rather than the operating system, then you'll need to visit the App Store instead:

1 Open the **App Store.**

2 Select **Updates** in the sidebar.

3 Either update individual apps, or click **Update All** in the top-right corner.

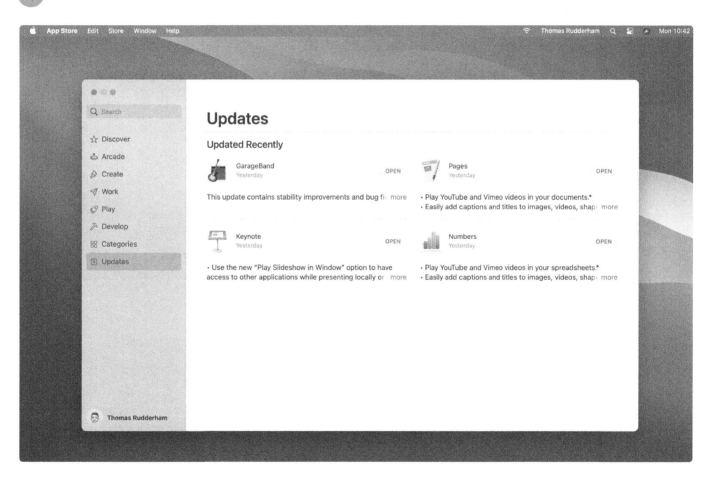

Use your iPad as a second screen

Use Sidecar to extend or mirror your desktop onto your iPad's touch display...

If you have an iPad released in 2018 or later, then you can use it to extend or mirror your Mac's display. There's no app to install, and everything works wirelessly (although you can plug your iPad into your Mac to keep its battery topped up). Apple calls this feature Sidecar, and it works by extending your Mac's display to one side. Think of it as extra screen space for you to place things. You can also mirror your Mac's display if needed, plus it's possible to use an Apple Pencil to tap and edit things that are placed on the iPad display. Here's how it works:

Extend or mirror your Mac desktop

1 Click the **AirPlay** icon in the Apple menu, then select your iPad. If you don't see the AirPlay icon, then open **System Preferences**, click **Sidecar**, then use the **Connect to** dropdown to select your iPad.

2 Your iPad should now show an extended part of your desktop. You can drag windows onto it and use it like a second monitor.

3 Another way to move windows (and apps) to the iPad is to hover the cursor over on the green fullscreen button in the top-left corner of a window/app, then choose **Move to my iPad**. The window or app will instantly appear on the iPad and be perfectly formatted to fit its display.

4 To mirror your Mac's screen, rather than extend it, click on the **AirPlay** icon in the Apple menu (which now looks like a blue rectangle), and choose **Mirror**.

5 To finish extending your desktop, click on the **AirPlay** icon and choose **Disconnect**. Alternatively, you can tap the **Disconnect** button on your iPad's display.

Sidebar controls

Take a look at the sidebar on your iPad and you'll see a number of controls running down the side of the screen. Here's what each button means:

Tap this to show or hide the menu bar when viewing a window full screen.

This will show or hide the Mac's Dock on the iPad.

Touch and hold to set the **Command** key. Double-tap to lock the key.

Touch and hold to set the **Option** key. Double-tap to lock the key.

Touch and hold to set the **Control** key. Double-tap to lock the key.

Touch and hold to set the **Shift** key. Double-tap to lock the key.

Undo the last action. Some apps will support multiple undos.

Display an on-screen keyboard.

Disconnect your iPad from the Mac.

Use an Apple Pencil to edit things

If you have an Apple Pencil with your iPad, then you can use it to draw, edit photos, sign documents, and manipulate objects. You can also use your Apple Pencil as a replacement for the mouse or trackpad to select things.

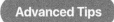
Use a monitor as a second screen

Give yourself some extra space to work with...

Plugging a monitor into your MacBook is actually a pretty good idea, because by using a second display it's possible to extend your desktop, mirror it and get a larger view, or run two fullscreen apps at once. Here's how to set up and use a second screen with your Mac...

1   Before you plug any screen into your Mac, check what ports it offers. Ideally, you should get a monitor with a Thunderbolt port, because this enables your Mac to send data to the monitor while also being powered by it. You also won't need an adapter.

2   If you have a monitor with Thunderbolt support, simply plug one end of a Thunderbolt cable into the monitor, then the other end into your Mac. It will instantly power up and connect.

Change the arrangement of your displays

If you're extending the desktop across both displays, and you want to drag files, folders, and windows from one screen to another, then you need to have them arranged properly in System Preferences. To do this:

1 Open **System Preferences** then click **Displays**.

2 Click on the **Arrangement** tab. You'll see a simplified graphic of the two displays. To work out which one is which, click and hold on a monitor. A red border will then appear around both the graphic and the monitor.

3 To move the new monitor to the left, right, above, or below your MacBook display, simply drag the new monitor and place it in the correct position.

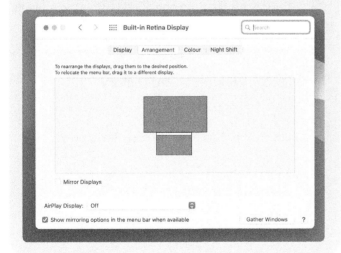

Move the Dock and menu bar between monitors

When you work with multiple displays, one will need to act as the 'main' display and show the Dock and menu bar. To set the main monitor:

1 Open **System Preferences** then click **Displays**.

2 Click **Arrangement**. Look for the white bar running along the top of a monitor graphic. This represents the main display.

3 To change the main display, click and hold on the white bar, then drag it to the other monitor.

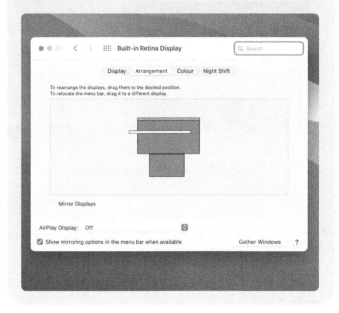

Mirror the displays

If you'd like to mirror your MacBook screen onto the monitor, then open **System Preferences**, click **Displays**, click **Arrangement**, then click **Mirror Displays**.

137

Use an eGPU to play the latest games

Get the latest graphics and fastest frame-rates...

So you're playing the latest games on your MacBook (such as Tomb Raider), but you're noticing that it's a little bit jerky at times. Help is at hand, if you have deep pockets. That's because any MacBook released during 2018 or later will support eGPUs, also known as external graphics cards. They look something like this:

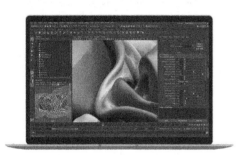

The Blackmagic eGPU Pro

With an eGPU plugged into your Mac, you can:

- Play the latest games with better graphics and frame rates.
- Render CGI and 3D content faster.
- Connect additional external monitors into your Mac.
- Use VR headsets plugged into the eGPU.
- Connect more than one eGPU using the multiple Thunderbolt 3 (USB-C) ports on your Mac.
- View the activity levels of built-in and external GPUs. To do this, open **Activity Monitor**, then choose **Window** > **GPU History**.

At the time of writing (September 2020), here's a list of recommended eGPU chassis that you can use to power an external graphics cards with your Mac:

- Blackmagic eGPU and Blackmagic eGPU Pro4
- Gigabyte RX 580 Gaming Box4
- Sonnet Radeon RX 570 eGFX Breakaway Puck
- Sonnet Radeon RX 560 eGFX Breakaway Puck5

And here's a list of recommended graphics cards that will work with these chassis:

- AMD Radeon RX 470
- AMD Radeon RX 480
- AMD Radeon RX 570
- AMD Radeon RX 580
- Radeon Pro WX 7100
- AMD Radeon RX Vega 56

Each eGPU chassis and graphics card has its own installation method, but in short, you'll need to insert the graphics card into the eGPU chassis, then plug the chassis into a Thunderbolt 3 port on your Mac. Next, open **System Preferences**, choose **Displays**, then choose the **Arrangement** tab. Next, drag the white menu bar to the box that represents the display attached to the eGPU. Now you're good to go.

If you need to disconnect the eGPU at any time, simply click on the **GPU** icon in the upper-right corner of the menu bar, then select **Disconnect "GPU name"**.

Activity Monitor

See what apps are draining battery, processor speed and RAM...

You might not know it, but your Mac is constantly performing dozens, maybe even hundreds of background tasks. Nearly all of these are key to running your Mac, and they only take up a fraction of memory and processing power.

Take "WindowServer" for example. It's a core part of macOS, and a liaison between your applications and the display. It's always running, and uses approximately 0.6% of the CPU, and around 9.5MB of RAM, but this can fluctuate wildly depending on how many apps and windows you have open.

To find Activity Monitor, open **LaunchPad** or click on **Go** in the Finder menu, then choose **Applications**. Next, click on **Utilities** and double-click on the **Activity Monitor** app.

See which application is using resources

Along the top of the Activity Monitor window, you'll five tabs. These let you see which apps are using the most processing power, memory, energy, hard drive data and network bandwidth.

If you're worried that a particular app is using all your Mac's processing power, click on the **CPU** tab, then click on the **% CPU** column to sort results. The application using the most CPU power will now appear at the top. As you can see in the screenshot below, in this example Activity Monitor is using the most CPU power:

Process Name	% CPU	CPU Time	Threads	Idle Wake-Ups	Kind	% GPU	GPU
Activity Monitor	42.0	2.67	11	7	Intel	0.0	
nsurlsessiond	11.5	31.86	10	1	Intel	0.0	
cloudd	4.3	17.58	10	4	Intel	0.0	
Finder	1.5	12.63	8	1	Intel	0.0	
cloudphotod	0.5	3.73	8	1	Intel	0.0	
cfprefsd	0.4	1.26	2	0	Intel	0.0	
Wi-Fi	0.4	0.63	6	0	Intel	0.0	

Force quit a process

If a process or app has crashed, then you can force quit it by selecting the process, then clicking the small **X** icon in the upper-left corner of the Activity Monitor window.

Be careful which processes you quit, however, as some are key to running your Mac. Force quit the wrong process and you might crash the entire operating system!

Recover Deleted Files

How to track down missing photos and files...

It happens to all of us at some point. Maybe we delete a photo by accident, override a file, or even wipe a portable storage device, then later realise we needed it after all. Thankfully, there are a number of ways you can recover deleted files and photos.

Recover deleted photos in the Photos app

This one's easy. If you've deleted an image in the Photos app, just click on the **Recently Deleted** shortcut in the sidebar. Anything you've deleted in the last 30 days will be there. Simply select the photo, then click the blue **Recover** button to restore the image.

Use Time Machine to revert or recover deleted items

If you've set up Time Machine, then you can use it to revert to an earlier version of a file or recover deleted items from your hard drive. To recover a deleted file using Time Machine:

1 Open the folder or location where you last saved the file.

2 Open the **Time Machine** app using Launchpad.

3 Use the arrows and timeline to browse the folder's history. As you go further back in time, the correct file should eventually appear.

4 Select the file or folder you want to recover, then click **Restore**.

Use third-party apps to recover deleted files

If you don't have Time Machine set up and need to recover deleted files from your Mac, then you're going to need third-party tools. They're never free, and there are lots to choose from, including File Salvage, Disk Drill, and Data Rescue 4. For this tutorial, we're going to use Mac Data Recovery Guru. You can download it from: http://goo.gl/WJQreY

Start by downloading Mac Data Recovery Guru. There's a free demo available, which lets you search your Mac or external storage devices for deleted items. To recover them, then you need to register.

Once downloaded and unzipped, drag the application file to your Applications folder, then open it. Use the sidebar to select the drive you wish to search, click **Start Scan**, then enter your administrator password to begin.

Mac Data Recovery Guru will scan your chosen drive for deleted files. It might take a while, so be patient. Once it has completed, you'll see a list of file types in the main panel to the right. Click on one, and a preview of it will appear, like this:

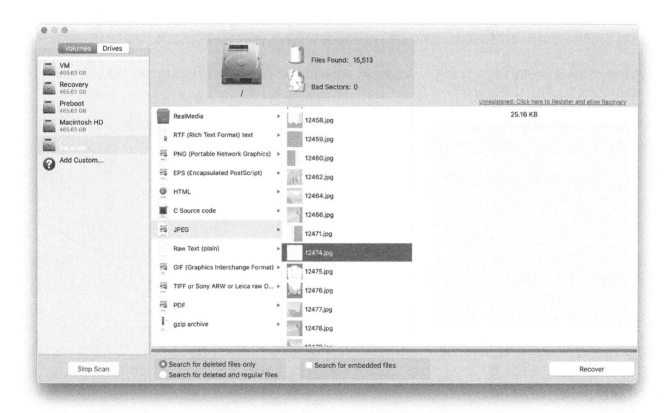

Once you've found the correct file to restore, click the **Recover** button at the bottom of the window. This will only appear once you have purchased the app. You can then choose where to save the file.

To recover more than one file at a time, hold down the **Command** button on your keyboard and click on the files. If you highlight the drive or volume, then everything is recovered at once.

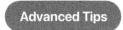
Format and Partition Drives

Learn how to erase hard drives and USB sticks...

Every now and then you might need to wipe a hard drive or a USB stick, removing all the data and information stored within it. If you've never done this before, then it might sound like a complicated task, but macOS includes a helpful app called Disk Utility which makes the job quick and simple.

Erase a drive or USB stick

Begin by making sure the drive you wish to format is plugged into your Mac. If it's an internal drive, then you're good to go. If it's a USB stick, just plug it into your Mac and wait for the drive to appear on the desktop.

Next, open the Disk Utility app. To find it, click the **Launchpad** icon in the dock, click on the **Other** folder, then click on the **Disk Utility** app icon.

After Disk Utility has opened, select the disk you wish to format using the left-hand menu, then click the **Erase** button in the toolbar at the top of the window.

You'll be asked which file format you wish to use. 'Mac OS Extended (Journaled)' is the Mac's native format. Choose this if you'd like to create a bootable drive, or if you know you will only ever use the drive on a Mac. 'MS-DOS (FAT)' is a widely used file format for both Macs and Windows PCs, but it's limited to file sizes of up to 4GB in size. 'ExFAT' doesn't have this limitation, but it's not widely supported by legacy media players.

Whichever format you choose, give it a name then click the **Erase** button. Disk Utility will then erase the drive, and re-mount it on the Desktop.

Partition a drive

Think of partitioning a drive as like cutting up a cake. You're basically taking one chunk of available data on a drive, then cutting it up into smaller pieces. By doing this you can use a separate partition to store files, or even install a bootable operation system.

Before you partition any drive, make sure you have a backup of any data already installed on it. This ensures you don't lose any important information if something goes wrong. Once you've backed up your data, open the **Disk Utility** app, then select the drive you wish to partition using the left-hand menu.

Next, click the **Partition** button in the toolbar at the top of the screen, then click the plus button below the overview.

You can now specify how much space the new partition should take up. You can do this by clicking and dragging the resize control, or you can specify exactly how big the partition should be by typing it's size in the GB text field.

You can also specify the file format you wish to use (see previous tutorial for the different types of file format available).

Once you're ready to create the partition, click **Apply**, and the drive will be partitioned, then become immediately accessible in the Finder to use how you want.

A new partition will behave just like a new hard drive. You can copy or save files to it, eject it, mount it, format it, and create more partitions within it.

Resize a partition

If you need more space within a partition, or want to return some space to another partition, begin by making a backup of all the data on the drive, then open **Disk Utility**. Next, select the drive using the left-hand menu, click on the **Partitions** button, then drag the dividing bar between existing partitions to resize the partitions as needed.

Delete a partition

If you need to remove a partition at any time, begin by making a backup of the entire drive, then:

1. Open **Disk Utility**.

2. Select the drive using the left-hand menu.

3. Click **Partition**.

4. Select the partition you wish to use.

5. Click the **minus** button, rather than the plus button, then click **Apply** for delete the partition.

Extend your MacBook Battery Life

Keep the battery going for a little longer with these helpful tips…

The battery within your MacBook is intended to last all day on one charge, which is pretty impressive when you consider the amount of technology packed within it. However, if you're planning to spend a lot of time away from a plug socket, then there are some clever ways to try and extend your MacBook's battery life.

Before we get to that, it's important to note that all batteries used in electronic devices such as your MacBook lose their ability to hold a full charge over time. This isn't a cynical ploy to encourage you to upgrade to a new device, but rather a result of the current technology used in batteries worldwide. Each time a battery discharges 85% of its capacity, then re-charges to 100%, is considered one charge cycle. It is suggested that every MacBook will lose 20% of its battery capacity after 1,000 charge cycles. That means if you re-charge your Mac every day you can expect to lose half the original battery capacity after 2-3 years. If you leave it plugged in most of the time, then it will last a lot longer.

With that out of the way, let's take a look at some of this things you can do to extend your MacBook's battery life:

Dim the display

The screen of your MacBook is one of the biggest drains of battery, so lower its brightness to extend the length of time you can run without a source of power. To adjust the brightness, you can either use the brightness slider on the Touch Bar, or via the **Displays** panel in **System Preferences**.

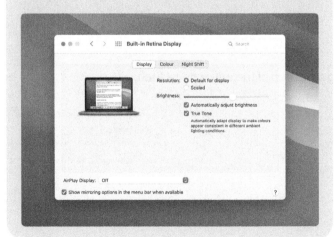

See if any apps are using energy

If you suspect an app is using lots of battery, just click the **battery** icon in the Apple menu at the top of the screen. Any apps using significant energy to run will be listed in the drop-down menu.

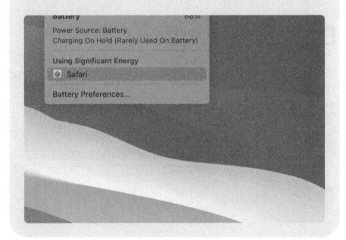

Disable Power Nap

Your Mac will periodically check for new emails, calendar events, and other iCloud updates, even even it's asleep. Admittedly this doesn't use a significant amount of energy, but if you'd like to save a small amount of battery life, then open **System Preferences**, click on **Battery** in the sidebar, then untick **Enable Power Nap while on battery power**.

Turn off Location Services

A handful of apps and services use Location Services to see your current position. Siri, for example, can use your location to find nearby restaurants. You can save a small amount of battery life by turning Location Services off. To do this:

1. Open **System Preferences**.

2. Select **Security & Privacy.**

3. Click the **Privacy** tab.

4. Click the **padlock** icon.

5. Uncheck **Enable Location Services**.

145

Troubleshooting

What to do when something goes wrong...

Macs are incredibly reliable machines, and surprisingly free from viruses and hacking too, but even so, things can go wrong occasionally. That's because they're amongst the most complicated machines ever created, with miniaturised components that are nanometres in size, include dozens of sensors, and process millions of lines of software code. Throw in third-party apps, unpredictable environments, and physical damage, and something might go wrong.

If the worst does happen; such as a frozen screen, a crashing app, or a loss of battery life, then you don't always need to call the Genius Bar to get it fixed. Instead, there are a number of things you can try first to try and remedy the situation. Let's take a look at some of the things you can try when something goes wrong:

How to fix a frozen app

If an application freezes and won't close, macOS provides an easy way to force-quit it.

1 Click on the **Apple** logo in the menu bar, then choose **Force Quit**. If the menu has also frozen then you can try pressing **Command** > **Option** > **Escape** on the keyboard.

2 In the Force Quit window, look for the app which has crashed. It should say (*not responding*) in grey text. Select it then click the **Force Quit** button to close the app.

Use Disk Utility to scan for problems

If you suspect that something is wrong with your Mac's hard drive, then you can use Disk Utility to check for problems, and even fix them for you.

1 To find Disk Utility, open **Launchpad** from the Dock, click on the folder called **Other**, then click on **Disk Utility**.

2 Click on the drive you wish to check, then click **First Aid**. The app will then check for any problems with the drive, and if necessary fix them.

3 Try using the Recovery Drive app. To do this force your Mac to turn off by holding down the **Power** button, then turn it back on while holding down the **option** button. Select **Recovery HD**, then press **Enter** to boot it. If your Mac loads, use the Apple menu to restart it the normal way. Hopefully, everything will be okay this time.

How to force your Mac to restart

If your Mac has become completely unresponsive, press and hold the **power** button for a few seconds and it will restart. If you're not sure, the power button is the small black square in the top-right corner of the keyboard.

How to fix a Mac that won't turn on

If your Mac won't finish starting up, or won't boot at all, then there are some simple things you can try:

1. Make sure it's plugged in. This might sound silly, but if the power cable was unplugged or the wall switch was turned off, then your MacBook's battery might have drained without you knowing.

2. Try unplugging then replugging the power cord. Sometimes it becomes loose.

3. Try using the Recovery Drive app. To do this force your Mac to turn off by holding down the **Power** button, then turn it back on while holding down the **option** button. Select **Recovery HD**, then press **Enter** to boot it. If your Mac loads, use the Apple menu to restart it the normal way. Hopefully, everything will be okay this time.

4. If none of the above works, then it's time to call the Genius Bar at your local Apple Store and make an appointment to get your Mac looked at (see across the page for more details).

How to reset the NVRAM

The NVRAM stores information about your Mac's screen resolution, speaker volume, startup disk and time. If you're having problems with any of these, then it's a good idea to reset the NVRAM. To do this:

1. Turn off your Mac. Turn it back on, and when you hear the startup chime press and hold the **Command** > **Option** > **P** > **R** keys.

2. If you've pressed the right keys, then your Mac will restart once more. You can now let go of the keys.

After your Mac finishes starting up, make sure to open System Preferences and adjust any settings that were reset, such as the sound volume, display resolution, startup disk, or time zone.

The Genius Bar

Get help when you need it most...

The Genius Bar is a technical support service in every Apple Store where you can get help to solve the problem or receive a replacement device.

They're often referred to as the heart and soul of an Apple Store. Every Genius Bar is manned by a team of technical specialists called "Geniuses". Each has experience solving every kind of hardware and software-related problems. They're also friendly and understanding to boot.

Are the team at the Genius Bar actually geniuses? Ask and you're likely to receive a shrug, a wink or a bemused look. But these dedicated guys and gals solve even the most complicated problems on a day-to-day basis. If they can't fix a problem with your Mac or iPhone, then no one else can.

Most services at the Genius Bar are carried out for free. Repairs are carried out in the store, often while you wait. If the Genius can't repair the device on the spot then a replacement is usually offered.

Booking a Genius Bar appointment

The easiest way to book a Genius Bar appointment is via the Apple Store website. The URL changes depending on your location, but Google search *"Book a Genius Bar appointment"* and the first result will take you to the right page. From the website you can select your nearest store and choose a suitable time and date – right down to the exact 10 minutes that suit your needs.

Please note that you'll need an Apple ID to book an appointment. This enables the Apple Genius to see your previous software and hardware purchases, which might prove to be helpful when diagnosing problems. It also makes paying for replacements and services much quicker.

Keep in mind that the Genius Bar is a popular service, so the first available appointment might be weeks in advance.

Attending the Genius Bar

Before going to the Genius Bar, make sure to fully backup your device. You can backup your Mac via Time Machine or iCloud. Both methods save all your apps, text messages, photos, contacts, settings and more. These can be transferred to the new Mac once it's activated.

If you've never walked into an Apple Store then worry not. They're designed to be easy to understand and navigate. That is if the throngs of crowds aren't in your way. The front of the store is laid out with wooden tables with the most recent devices available to test and play with. Further back you'll see Macs and accessories, and on the back wall is the Genius Bar. If the store is configured in a different way (for example it has multiple rooms/halls), then look for the long wooden bench with black stools in front of it.

You check in with an employee holding a blue iPad. Can't see them through the crowd? Look for any other employee in a blue shirt, they'll be able to help. Alternatively, you can check in using the Apple Store app, but being met face-to-face is always more reassuring.

Once you're at the Genius Bar be polite and explain the problem with your device. The Genius team interview dozens of customers each day, sometimes hundreds. It's likely they've encountered every kind of problem, whether hardware or software related, and should be able to quickly identify what's wrong with a device. Research shows that a smile and positive attitude is the best way to get good customer service, and that applies to both employee and customer. Whereas creating a scene might get you thrown out of the store by security, a friendly chat could get you a free repair or additional advice.

Index A-N

Quickly find what you're looking for...

Index N-W

Quickly find what you're looking for...

Made in the USA
Monee, IL
14 December 2020